SO-BYF-363

CURRENT ISSUES BIBLE STUDY SERIES

Islam

CHRISTIANITYTODAY

INTERNATIONAL

THOMAS NELSON

Since 1798

NASHVILLE   DALLAS   MEXICO CITY   RIO DE JANEIRO   BEIJING

Current Issues Bible Study Series: Islam
Copyright © 2008 Christianity Today International

All rights reserved. No portion of this book may be reproduced, stored in a retrieval
system, or transmitted in any form or by any means—electronic, mechanical, photocopy,
recording, scanning, or other—except for brief quotations in critical reviews or articles,
without the prior written permission of the publisher.

Published in Nashville, Tennessee, by Thomas Nelson. Thomas Nelson is a registered
trademark of Thomas Nelson, Inc.

Thomas Nelson, Inc. titles may be purchased in bulk for educational, business,
fundraising, or sales promotional use. For information, please e-mail SpecialMarkets@
thomasnelson.com.

Unless otherwise indicated, Scripture taken from the New Century Version. Copyright ©
2005 by Thomas Nelson, Inc. Used by permission. All rights reserved.

Scripture quotations marked NIV are from the HOLY BIBLE: NEW INTERNATIONAL
VERSION®. © 1973, 1978, 1984 by International Bible Society. Used by permission of
Zondervan Publishing House. All rights reserved.
Scripture quotations marked MSG are from *The Message* by Eugene H. Peterson. © 1993,
1994, 1995, 1996, 2000. Used by permission of NavPress Publishing Group. All rights
reserved.
Scripture quotations marked NKJV are from THE NEW KING JAMES VERSION. © 1982
by Thomas Nelson, Inc. Used by permission. All rights reserved.
Scripture quotations marked NRSV are from the NEW REVISED STANDARD VERSION
of the Bible. © 1989 by the Division of Christian Education of the National Council of the
Churches of Christ in the U.S.A. All rights reserved.

Editor: Kelli B. Trujillo
Development Editors: Kelli B. Trujillo and Roxanne Wieman
Associate Editor: JoHannah Reardon
Review Editor: David Neff
Page Designer: Robin Crosslin

ISBN-13: 978-1-4185-3424-0

Printed in the United States of America
08 09 10 11 12 RRD 6 5 4 3 2 1

CONTENTS

CONTRIBUTING WRITERS

Miriam Adeney is editor at large for *Christianity Today* and is associate professor of world Christian studies at Seattle Pacific University.

James A. Beverley is professor of theology and ethics at Tyndale Seminary in Toronto. He is author of *Understanding Islam*.

Chris Blumhofer is associate editor of BuildingChurchLeaders.com, a Christianity Today International Web site devoted to equipping church leaders.

Jonathan Bonk is the executive director of the Overseas Ministries Study Center, editor of the *International Bulletin of Mission Research*, and project director for the *Dictionary of African Christian Biography*.

Elesha Coffman is a graduate student in religion at Duke University. She was formerly the managing editor of *Christian History* magazine.

Stan Guthrie is managing editor of special projects for *Christianity Today*.

Warren Larson is director of the Zwemer Center for Muslim Studies at Columbia International University, Columbia, South Carolina.

Dan Lentz is director of the Small Group Network, a network of small group leaders, churches, small group resource providers, and other Christian organizations.

Anthony McRoy is an Islamic studies expert, religion journalist, and a lecturer at the Evangelical Theological College of Wales.

Sheikh Omar Bakri Muhammad is the leader of one of the most controversial Islamist groups in the U.K., *Al Muhajiroun* (which means "the emigrants" in Arabic).

Brandon O'Brien is assistant editor of *Leadership* and a former pastor of two small congregations in rural Arkansas.

Eric Reed is editor-in-chief of the Consumer Media Group at Christianity Today International and former managing editor of *Leadership*.

"Rockie" is a former Muslim; at the time her article was written, she was a student majoring in biblical studies.

Lamin Sanneh, a former Muslim, is the D. Willis James Professor of Missions and World Christianity and professor of history at Yale Divinity School.

Alison Tarka is a stay-at-home mom, blogger, violinist, and freelance writer for small group studies. Alison once lived and studied in the Middle East; she currently lives in Portland, Oregon.

Jason Tarka is a pastor in Portland, Oregon where he leads worship, teaches theology, writes for small groups, and enjoys the best coffee in the country.

Kelli B. Trujillo is a writer, editor, and adult ministry leader at her church.

William H. Willimon is Dean of the Chapel and professor of Christian Ministry, Duke University, Durham, North Carolina.

Wendy Murray Zoba is a senior writer for *Christianity Today* and the author of several books, including *On Broken Legs: A Shattered Life, a Search for God, a Miracle That Met Me in a Cave in Assisi.*

INTRODUCTION

It's the inevitable topic discussed on the evening news: Islam. Whether it's a report on conflict in the Middle East, comments about "Islamic extremists" from national politicians, reports of racial profiling or hate crimes against American Muslims, protests against the incarceration of Muslims captured as part of the "War on Terror," or details of another terror-plot uncovered, Islam—and its beliefs—are becoming a central part of our national vocabulary. And as we absorb the images and rhetoric on Islam bombarding us from TV, radio, and the Internet, we form opinions about Muslims and what they believe.

But are our opinions right? Are they grounded in an accurate understanding of Islamic belief? And further, how are our opinions and ideas about Islam informed by our Christian faith?

This *Current Issues Bible Study* guide is designed to facilitate lively and engaging discussion on various facets of this topic and how it connects to our lives as Jesus's followers. As you explore the topic of Islam together, we hope this *Current Issues Bible Study* guide will help you grow closer as a group and challenge you in ways you may not expect.

For Small Groups

These studies are designed to be used in small groups—communities of people with a commitment to and connection with each other. Whether you're an existing small group or you're just planning to meet for the next eight weeks, this resource will help you deepen in your personal faith and grow closer with each other.

Along with the eight studies, you'll find a bonus Small-Group Builder article from *Christianity Today*'s SmallGroups.Com (www.smallgroups.com). On Smallgroups.com, you'll find everything you need to successfully run a small-groups ministry. The insightful free articles and theme-specific downloads provide expert training. The reproducible curriculum courses bring thought leaders from across the world into your group's discussion at a fraction of the price. And the revolutionary SmallGroupsConnect social network will help keep your group organized and connected 24/7.

Christianity Today Articles

Each study session begins with one or two thought-provoking articles from *Christianity Today* or one of its sister publications. These articles are meant to help you dive deeply into the topic and engage with a variety of thoughts and opinions. Be sure to read the articles before you arrive to your small group meeting; the time you invest on the front end will greatly enrich your group's discussion. As you read, you may find the articles persuasive and agree heartily with their conclusions; other times you may disagree with the claims of an article, but that's great too. We want these articles to serve as a springboard for lively discussion, so differences in opinion are welcome.

Timing

These studies are designed to be flexible, with plenty of discussion, activities, and prayer time to fill a full small group meeting. If you'd like, you can zero in on a few questions or teaching points and discuss them in greater depth, or you can aim to spend a few minutes on each question of a given session. Be sure to manage your time so that you're able to spend time on the "Going Forward" questions and prayer time at the end of each study.

Ground Rules

True spiritual growth happens in the context of a vibrant Christian community. To establish that type of community in your small group, we recommend a few ground rules:

- Guarantee confidentiality. Promise together that whatever is said in the context of your small group meeting is kept in that small group meeting. This sense of trust and safety will enable you to more honestly share about your spiritual struggles.

- Participate—with balance. We all have different personalities. Some of us like to talk . . . a lot. Others of us prefer to be quiet. But for this study to truly benefit your group, everyone needs to participate. Make it a personal goal to answer (aloud) at least half of the discussion questions in a given session. This will allow space for others to talk (lest you dominate discussion too much) but will also guarantee your own contribution is made to the discussion (from which other group members will benefit).

• Be an attentive listener—to each other and to God. As you read Scripture and discuss these important cultural issues, focus with care and love on the other members of your group. These questions are designed to be open-ended and to allow for a diversity of opinion. Be gracious toward others who express views that are different than your own. And even more important, prayerfully remain attentive to the presence of God speaking to and guiding your group through the Holy Spirit.

It is our prayer that this *Current Issues Bible Study* guide will change the lives of your group members as you seek to integrate your faith into the cultural issues you face every day. May the Holy Spirit work in and through your group as you challenge and encourage each other in spiritual growth.

What do Muslims believe

and how do their beliefs

affect Christ-followers?

SCRIPTURE FOCUS

Acts 17:16–34

1 Peter 3:13–18

UNDERSTANDING ISLAM

■

The radio show *This American Life* once tried to describe the lives of Muslims in America. The title of the segment was "Shouting Across the Divide," a clear allusion to the challenges that Muslims face living in a society where they are, at best, misunderstood and, at worst, unwelcome.

Christians who understand Islam know that the divide between our faiths is real. Muslims and Christians hold different beliefs on fundamental issues. Communicating despite our differences requires that we turn away from hostility and ignorance, seeking understanding instead.

Using Wendy Zoba's *Christianity Today* articles "Islamic Fundamentals" and "How Muslims See Christianity," we'll pursue a basic understanding of the world's second-largest (and fastest-growing) religion. We'll also consider how understanding Islam changes the way we relate to followers of Muhammad.

■ Before You Meet

Read "Islamic Fundamentals" and "How Muslims See Christianity" both by Wendy Murray Zoba from *Christianity Today*.

ISLAMIC FUNDAMENTALS

Christians have a responsibility to understand our Muslim neighbors and their beliefs

By Wendy Murray Zoba

Despite Islam's diversity throughout its history, the role of the Prophet Muhammad and the place of the Qur'an have remained unchallenged.

The Role of Muhammad

For Muslims, Muhammad is the last and greatest of the Prophets, surpassing Jesus. He was born in AD 570 in Mecca (in what is today Saudi Arabia). Mecca's heart of worship at the time was the local Ka'bah (shrine), or the Black Stone, and its numerous idols. According to Islamic tradition, Abraham's firstborn son Ishmael and Ishmael's mother Hagar, after being banished by Sarah, ended up in the desert surrounding Mecca, where they were miraculously rescued. Abraham—or Ibrahim, as he is known in Arabic—visited them there and he and Ishmael built the Ka'bah. Muslims believe they are the true heirs, through Ishmael, to the promise God made to Abraham. Jesus and Mary were among the many images—in addition to the goddesses of fertility and power—worshiped at the Ka'bah during Muhammad's day.

Muhammad learned about "the People of the Book"—Jews and Christians—in his youth. He felt troubled that his own people, the Arabs, did not have a book of their own. As he reflected despondently on this one day in a cave on Mount Hira (in AD 609 or 610), Muhammad said the angel Gabriel appeared to him: "Recite: In the Name of thy Lord who created Man of a blood-clot. Recite: And thy Lord is the Most Generous, who taught by the pen, taught Man that he knew not" (Surah 96:1–4). The injunction to "recite" meant "make vocal what is already written," says Islamicist Kenneth Cragg, which means it was the "send-ing down" of a preexistent book. (Qur'an is Arabic for "recitation.") At first Muhammad feared he had been overtaken by a jinn, a troubling spirit. But Muhammad's wife Khadijah encouraged him that his visions were indeed from God and that he had been chosen as his special mes-senger. Muhammad's fear gave way to acquiescence and the visions recurred with greater frequency.

His recitations denounced idol worship and proclaimed the total sovereignty of the One True God. Because the People of the Book also claimed allegiance to this God, his early recitations about Christianity and Judaism in the Qur'an were irenic: "O believers, be you God's help-ers, as Jesus, Mary's son, said to the Apostles. 'Who will be my help-ers unto God?' The Apostles said, 'We will be helpers of God' " (Surah 61:14). His small circle of followers, composed mostly of family mem-bers and domestic help, became increasingly assertive in their belief that Muhammad was a prophet, and this aroused the consternation of the people of Mecca, many of whom felt their vested interests in idol worship and commerce were threatened.

The deaths of his beloved wife Khadijah (fifteen years his senior) and his uncle Abu Talib (who also served as a protector) in 619 precipi-tated a crisis for Muhammad. He and his followers could stay in Mecca in perpetual jeopardy as a despised minority, or he could move to a new location where the fledgling faith could gain a foothold and grow. Some of his disciples had succeeded in their missionary undertakings to the north, in a place called Yathrib, later called Medina. So in 622, Muhammad migrated to that city to form a new base of activity. The famous *hijrah* (emigration) occurred in September of that year and be-came the historical fulcrum of Islam.

Several things happened with this move that solidified and rede-fined Islam. First, despite the previous missionary successes in Medina, Muhammad's new religion hardly received unanimous affirmation upon his arrival. Some resisted his presumption and others eschewed the no-tion of converting. Second, Muhammad had anticipated a warm recep-tion from the People of the Book—primarily the Jews—in Medina, since they too were "Scripture people." Instead they treated him with "amused disdain," says Cragg, and rejected his claims as "pretentious."

These difficulties triggered a shift in Muhammad's message. The portions of the Qur'an "sent down" during this period took on a more aggressive political and legal tone, in contrast to its previous poetic and mystical reflections. During the Medinan years (622 – 630) Muhammad consolidated Islam into a functioning, overarching political and religious community—the *umma*—and built a mosque. He also fashioned his revelations into principles, and administered the social, political, economic, and religious affairs of the Medinans. Recitations regarding the People of the Book (both Jews and Christians) became more belligerent: "God fight them, what liars they are" (Surah 9:30); and "O believers, take not Jews and Christians as friends; they are friends of each other. Whoso of you makes them his friends is one of them. God guides not the people of the evildoers" (Surah 5:56).

At the same time, hostilities with the Meccans continued as Muhammad raided their caravans traveling north. The Battle of Badr (624) proved decisive for establishing Islam as an aggressive force. "[T]he sword was unleashed and the scabbard cast away. The *jihad*, or appeal to battle, had been irrevocably invoked," Cragg says. (Jihad also has a spiritual sense in Islam: the struggle of the self against veering from the truth.) A contentious debate continues today in Muslim circles about whether this aggression should be considered "defensive," since the future of Islam was at stake. The Qur'an maintains that war is an evil, but the extinction of Islam is a greater evil (Surah 2:217). But for all intents and purposes, the victory at Badr marked a critical stage in the evolution of Islam from a defensive to an offensive position.

By 630 Muhammad returned to Mecca in victory. He claimed the city for Islam and destroyed the idols being worshiped at the Ka'bah. This action introduced the notion of "manifest success"—geographical dominance—as a validating sign of Islam.

Muhammad "combined the good and the bad qualities of an Oriental chief," notes Christian historian Philip Schaff. He despised ostentation and lived in small mud-brick cottages with his many wives. He mended his own clothes, cobbled his shoes, milked goats, and was accessible, gracious, and hospitable to visitors. Muhammad died in 632, two years after the conquest of Mecca. The recitations were complete—the canon, so to speak, was closed.

The Qur'an

The Qur'an to the Muslim is not what the Bible is to the Christian. Rather, the Qur'an is to the Muslim what *Jesus* is to the Christian. Jesus is the Word made flesh and the Qur'an, for the Muslim, is the Word made text. The Book preexisted in heaven before Muhammad received the command to recite and he simply brought into physical being what already existed in completeness. To borrow Christian vocabulary, one might say he incarnated the Book. Muhammad was illiterate, according to Islamic tradition, ensuring the purity of the revelation (though some, including Cragg, dispute that view). When the recitations ended with Muhammad's death in 632, points in the Qur'an required further clarification for long-term communal guidance. This clarification gave rise to Tradition (hadith sharif): the collected sayings, thoughts, and deeds of Muhammad. Muslims looked to how Muhammad lived for guidance in practical living. For example, Al-Ghazali—an eleventh-century Muslim legal scholar and equivalent of Thomas Aquinas—wrote:

Know that the key of happiness is . . . imitating God's Apostle in all his goings out and comings in, in his movements and times of quiescence, even in the manner of his eating, his deportment, his sleep and his speech. . . . So you must sit while putting on trousers and stand while putting on a turban: You must begin with the right foot when putting on your sandals, and eat with your right hand: When cutting your nails you must begin with the forefinger of the right hand and finish with the thumb: in the foot you must begin with the little toe of the right foot and finish with the little toe of the left.

"God does not speak in a vacuum," says Dr. Mahmoud Ayoub, a Muslim and professor of Islamic studies and comparative religion at Temple University. "God speaks to people in their own situation. So there is a human dimension of the Qur'an." Even so, Muslims do not regard the Qur'an as a historical document to be reinterpreted in new contexts and eras. "It's a miracle of speech," Ayoub says. "But we cannot apply the principles of biblical criticism to the Qur'an. There is no evolution of the text."

Consequences of Their Faith

This notion of an immutable text has been put to the test as Islam has moved West. An example of how the Qur'an has collided with Western sensibilities is in its statements about women. In Muhammad's time, women's roles were notably inferior to men's. One of the most difficult verses reads: "Righteous women are therefore obedient, guarding the secret for God's guarding. And those you fear may be rebellious admonish; banish them to their couches, and beat them" (Surah 4:34). In matters of inheritance, women are to receive half of what men receive (Surah 4:11). Men are the "managers" of women (Surah 4:35) and can "come unto [their] tillage as they wish" (sexually) (Surah 2:223); can divorce their wives by stating "I divorce you" three times (2:229–230); and may take more than one wife (4:29). "What is happening now is that a lot of Islamic scholars are trying to extricate Islam from that culture," says Jane Smith, professor of Islamic studies at Hartford Seminary in Connecticut and author of *Islam in America*. "Many are increasingly saying we must look to the particular time and to the particular context."

Many feminist scholars look to Muhammad's example—he affirmed and empowered women—as a means of interpreting these troubling passages. From this vantage, many see these verses as strangely empowering for women. Inheritance, these scholars argue, is not earned and so is not a right. Given that men are responsible for the well-being of the families and women are not, that they receive anything at all is a reflection of their esteemed status. The division of roles, wherein men "manage" the affairs of women, is actually liberating. One noted feminist scholar, a Western convert to Islam, says that this arrangement "accords with the God-given natures of men and women."

The surahs (chapters) regarding polygamy and divorce are trickier, but also not without merit, some would argue. Many contemporary Muslim scholars say polygamy ensures that men will not take on mistresses and bear illegitimate children, and grants these other women legal protection. A woman without a husband in a Muslim community is in an insecure position, and since there are usually more women than men, polygamy ensures companionship to them all. "To share a husband is better than having none," Napoleon John writes in *Partners or Prisoners*, citing Hammudah Abdalati, author of *Islam in Focus*. "If [the husband] is bound to be monogamous, this may lead to hypocrisy, adultery, illegitimacy, abortion, and many other troubles."

The triple pronouncement of divorce offers the needed restraints to prevent a proclamation in a heated moment. The same principle applies to the stages of discipline before a beating. A verbal reprimand must precede a wife's being banished from her husband's bed, which must precede being beaten. In other words, beating is a last resort. Both Jane Smith and *The New York Times* Book Review (in reviewing Smith's *Islam in America*) are surprisingly uncritical of such interpretations, given the outrage the Southern Baptists's "submission statement" elicited. "[N]o reputable Muslim interpreters would suggest it should involve anything more than the lightest of taps as a reminder to the wife of conjugal responsibilities," Smith writes. There are many happy Muslim marriages and loving husbands who do not beat their wives. But this discussion highlights the difficulties Muslims encounter in bringing their view of the Qur'an to the West.

Many women view marriage the same way Muslims view their relationship with God, says "Kaye," an American missionary in a Muslim country who does not want to be identified. A Muslim woman "sees marriage as a contract, and they're trying to work out their part of the contract to get to paradise. Sometimes they see being beaten as part of the contract." Muslims tend to look upon every relationship as a contract, says Kaye, "including their relationship to God."

Islam is a religion of duty and submission in which human effort leads to salvation rather than proceeds out of it. "There is no view of redemption, as such, for the Muslim," says Mahmoud Ayoub. "Adam is the first sinner, but also the first prophet. He missed the mark by disobeying the divine command, and he asked God's forgiveness. Every human is born like Adam, capable of knowing God and having pure faith. There is no original sin in Islam, only original purity."

In other words, we, like Adam, may miss the mark now and then. But we, also like Adam, have the capability to right ourselves and rehabilitate our standing before God, through submission and through the five pillars. The characteristic description for human status before God is 'abd—servant or slave. God, in his mercy, revealed himself through the Qur'an and his final prophet, but Islam nevertheless remains a religion driven by ongoing human efforts to earn God's favor.

HOW MUSLIMS SEE CHRISTIANITY

Many Muslims don't understand Christianity—especially the idea of salvation by grace through faith.

By Wendy Murray Zoba

The driving principle behind Islam, recited in the call to prayer, is *La ilaha illa Allah*—"There is no god but Allah." This is the lens through which Muslims interpret all other religious confessions, and it explains why many Muslims do not understand Christianity.

It seems that either no complete version of either Testament had been translated into Arabic in Muhammad's time or that he did not have access to the testaments. His references to Jesus and Mary in the Qur'an are sketchy, without any verbatim attributions. In addition, it is apparent that the Christians Muhammad knew were contentious and seemed confused: the Christianity Muhammad was exposed to was probably embroiled in a debate about the nature of Christ, leaving the impression that Christians mostly disagreed about what their faith meant. Given these factors, Muhammad's exposure to Christianity conjured up more confusion than elucidation.

There is no category in Islam for the One true God with a triune nature. "The Messiah, Jesus son of Mary, was only a Messenger of God, and His Word that He committed to Mary, and a Spirit from Him," the Qur'an says. "So believe in God and His Messengers, and say not, 'Three.' Refrain: better is it for you. God is only One God" (Surah 4:169). Muslims do not understand our Book: Why are there *four* gospels? Why does it include letters written to other people? Why is it written in Greek when Jesus spoke Aramaic? What kind of Scripture could this be, if God himself did not dictate it? The "sending down" of the New Testament Scriptures involved human instrumentality, so Muslims wonder how such a book, so handled, is divine revelation. Even more perplexing to them is the Christian understanding of *'Isa*—Jesus. Muhammad subordinated all other belief systems to the notion that he was the final prophet and the Qur'an the final message from God. Muhammad saw the Jesus of the Christians as an important prophet—along the lines of Noah, Abraham, and Moses—but not the Alpha and Omega.

Muslims honor Jesus and allow that miracles are associated with him, but they recoil at the notion of worshiping him. A prophet can be virgin-born, but not "Emmanuel—God with us." Muslims concur that Jesus was condemned to the cross, but they claim he was never crucified. The Qur'an asserts that "they did not slay him, neither crucified him, only a likeness of that was shown to them" (Surah 4:155).

Islam cannot conceive of either a prophet or a son who is executed as a criminal. If Jesus died on the cross, "enduring the shame," then from the Muslim perspective he utterly failed. Muhammad's victory, first in Medina and later in Mecca, validated his prophetic role. Manifest success became the measuring rod for authentic Sunni Islam (its major branch), and by that standard, Jesus failed. His mission was cut short without his realizing any real, measurable "success."

Jesus as God's son is even more problematic. A son is a privileged and pampered position, "which will not soil a hand lest the heir be mistaken for a menial slave," notes Cragg. So when Paul writes, "Though he was God, he . . . made himself nothing [and] took the humble position of a slave . . . dying a criminal's death on a cross" (Phil. 2:6–9), it's a losing proposition from the Muslim perspective. A son of God would never be a slave and would never die a criminal's death. "The logic by which, for the Qur'an, Jesus can never be 'Son' to God is precisely the logic by which, for Paul and the New Testament, he is," Cragg says. "Truly God is one God," the Qur'an says. "Glory be to Him and no 'son' to Him whose are all things in the heavens and the earth" (Surah 4:171). Without a concept of sonship and Jesus's atoning sacrifice on the cross, there is no remission of sins and therefore no grace. Mahmoud Ayoub says that "salvation by faith is arrogance—who decides?" To him it seems incomprehensible that a person would claim to be a servant of God without having to *do* anything. As one imam expressed it, "That is too good to be true!" The validating sign of faith, says Ayoub, is in what you *do*—not in what you cannot do, as is implicit in the notion of grace. This is a difficult concept for Muslims to grasp. In Islam, God is all merciful, all knowing, all compassionate—Muslims have ninety-nine names for what God is—but none conveys the intimacy of *abba* whom we approach in reconciliation by virtue of his saving grace.

The Challenge to the Church

This sense of religious duty and measurable human effort is, surprisingly, what attracts many Western converts to Islam. "I wanted a discipline to pattern my life by," writes one young woman, formerly a Christian, on a Web site that posts testimonies about conversions to Islam. "I did not just want to believe someone was my savior and through this I held the ticket to Heaven. I wanted to know how to act to receive the approval of God." Another former Christian who converted to Islam wrote: "As with many other Christians too, I had become disillusioned with the hypocrisy of the Church. . . . My attention was drawn towards the beliefs and practices of Islam."

But this works-oriented theology can cut the other way. Says Roy Oksnevad, director of the Institute of Muslim Studies at Wheaton College: "[O]ne former Muslim has said Islam had the rules and discipline she wanted in her life, but lacked the power to live the life the rules stipulated: 'As a system of personal discipline, Islam has few equals. As a means of earning God's favor, it's a spiritual treadmill.'" Another Web site posts testimonies by Muslim converts to Christianity. A man who identifies himself only as "a brother from Saudi Arabia" writes:

As a teenager I went to the mosque five times a day in obedience to my parents. . . . One night while I was asleep I had this horrible dream of me being taken into hell. What I saw there brought me real fear and these dreams kept coming to me almost every night. . . . Suddenly one day Jesus appeared to me and said, "Son, I am the way, the truth, and the life. And if you would give your life to Me and follow Me, I would save you from the hell that you have seen." . . . Christianity is totally banned in Saudi Arabia. . . . [After I converted] I was taken into custody and tortured. They told me I would be beheaded if I did not turn back to Islam. . . . I told the authorities I'm willing to die for Jesus and that I would never come back to Islam. . . . The appointed day came for my execution and I was waiting with much anticipation, yet very strong in my faith. . . . One hour lapsed, two hours went by, then it became three hours and then the day passed by. No one turned up. Then two days later the authorities turned and opened the doors and told me, "You demon! Get out from this place!"

In the course of writing this article, I kept confronting a contradiction. Many who are intimately acquainted with Muslims expressed concern about the missionary mandate of some to conquer the world for Islam. At the same time, people expressed genuine fondness, compassion, and good will for their Muslim friends and neighbors. David Echols of the South Asian Friendship Center says to look at it this way: there is the *Islamic system*, which is aggressive and intentional about its missiological work, and then there are *Muslims*—the people who work in Wal-Mart or live down the street. The latter are the people you will meet in the grocery store. They long to get close to God and to live as good Muslims. Many are lonely for friendships. It is on this human level that Christians will overcome the stereotypes about Muslims—and where Muslims will overcome their stereotypes about Christians. Only on the personal level will authentic witness be born between the two.

Wendy Murray Zoba is a senior writer for Christianity Today *and the author of several books, including* On Broken Legs: A Shattered Life, a Search for God, a Miracle That Met Me in a Cave in Assisi.

("Islamic Fundamentals" and "How Muslims See Christianity" were originally published online at www.christianitytoday.com in March 2000.)

For more insightful articles from *Christianity Today* magazine, visit http://www.ctlibrary.com/ and subscribe now.

■ Open Up

Select one of these activities to launch your discussion time.

Option 1

Discuss one of these icebreaker questions:

- Describe a time in which you were in a new place and didn't know "the rules" for how to behave in that context. What happened? How did you respond?

- Take a moment and think about a relationship that you have with someone who is very different from you—perhaps in his or her hobbies, personality, or beliefs. What's it like being in that relationship? How has it changed you?

Option 2

Many of us only know Islam from what we learn in the news media. In their portrayal, certain attributes of Islam stand out, while other attributes are ignored. Ask everyone in the group to write two standout characteristics of Islam on a sheet of paper. Mix all the papers together, and then have someone from the group read the responses aloud.

- Based on our responses, what are some terms we would use to characterize Islam?

- How would a Muslim doing the same exercise be likely to characterize Christianity?

■ The Issue

Peter exhorted the church to "Always be ready to answer everyone who asks you to explain about the hope you have" (1 Peter 3:15). We don't explain our hope in a vacuum, however; we do so in the context of many religions and worldviews. In order to effectively articulate the love of Christ, we must understand how Muslims understand their faith—where they place their hope, and how they live out their beliefs.

Take a moment and review "Islam 101: Basics of a Foreign Faith" (in the appendix on p.172).

- How would you summarize the major beliefs of Islam in your own words?

• How do these beliefs compare and contrast to the major beliefs of Christians?

■ Reflect

Read Acts 17:16–34 and 1 Peter 3:13–18 on your own. What attitudes and actions do these passages set forth as we consider our faith in light of other religions? What phrases rise to the surface? Take notes about what stands out to you.

■ Let's Explore

Christians must take steps to understand Islam.

Paul had a missionary's heart for the people of Athens. As he spent time in that city, he observed the religion the people practiced and the Bible says he was "greatly distressed" by what he saw. But rather than being driven to anger or polemics, Paul's distress motivated him to start conversations with the regular people of the city.

• Review Acts 17:16–34. What does Paul's distress demonstrate about his heart? How does it challenge or convict us as we think about reaching out to Muslims?

• Zoba writes, "Only on the personal level will authentic witness be born between [Muslims and Christians]." What prevents us as individuals from building relationships with Muslims? What changes would we need to make in our lives to build personal relationships with them?

Christians have a foundation on which to begin interacting with Muslims.

Acts 17:17 tells us that Paul "reasoned" (NIV) with the non-believers in Athens—implying that he worked to find common ground between their thought processes and his, between their belief systems and his. When Paul pushes his believers to consider the particularities of Christianity, he begins on their "turf," referring to an altar dedicated "To a God Who is Not Known."

- What are some of the beliefs that Christians and Muslims hold in common? (Refer to "Islam 101" in the appendix or to Zoba's "Islamic Fundamentals.") Does it surprise you to see these similarities? Why or why not?

- How does it make it harder to talk about Christianity to a Muslim, given that there are a noticeable amount of shared beliefs between the two faiths? How does it make it easier for us to talk about our faiths?

The fact that Muslims and Christians share beliefs that resemble each other does not mean that their differences are insignificant. In "How Muslims See Christianity," Zoba quotes Kenneth Cragg: "The logic by which, for the Qur'an, Jesus can never be 'Son' of God is precisely the logic by which, for Paul and the New Testament, he is."

- What are some of the essential beliefs of Christianity that make our faith categorically different from Islam? (Refer to the articles and share as many examples as you can find.)

- Why is it important to acknowledge both the similarities and the differences between our two faiths? What affect could such an acknowledgement have on our relationships with Muslims?

Christians must be able to give Muslims a reason for the hope they have.

- Read aloud 1 Peter 3:13–18. What are the convictions you hold and the experiences of your life that give you a reason to hope in Jesus Christ for salvation? Share from your personal experiences.

- In "How Muslims See Christianity," Zoba describes Islam as having a works-oriented theology. What does the New Testament teach about works-oriented theologies?

- How does your experience of the Christian faith (that is, "the hope you have") enable you to talk about faith and works? What might you say if you were talking with a Muslim friend about this issue?

■ Going Forward

Leadership journal published the results of a survey of Muslims who converted to Christianity. Interestingly, the reasons Muslims convert are not based on apologetic arguments or theological IQ as much as they are based on personal experiences and basic Christian beliefs. The top five reasons *Leadership* reported:

— The life style of Christians
— The power of God in answered prayer and healing
— Dissatisfaction with the type of Islam they had experienced
— The spiritual truth in the Bible
— Biblical teachings about the love of God
(Reported in *Leadership*, Winter 2008)

- Reflect on the list above. How might a Muslim witness these things in your life? How would you like to improve in the way you exemplify some of these ideas? Of the five areas above, which one in particular would you like to grow in your ability to live out or to speak about?

Now take some time to pray about what you've learned and the areas in which you want to develop. Commit your hearts, minds, and lifestyles to God, and ask that he would bring you into personal relationships with Muslims. If there are specific Muslims already known by members of the group, share their names and commit to pray for them both now and in the coming days.

■ Want to Explore More?

Recommended Resources

Answering Islam, 2nd ed.: The Crescent in Light of the Cross, Abdul Saleeb and Norman Geisler (Baker, 2002; ISBN 9780801064302)

Daughters of Islam: Building Bridges with Muslim Women, Miriam Adeney (InterVarsity Press, 2001; ISBN 9780830823451)

Is the Father of Jesus the God of Mohammed?, Timothy George (Zondervan, 2002; ISBN 9780310247487)

Islam: A Christian Introduction, Winfried Corduan (InterVarsity Press, 2001; ISBN 9780830849949)

Sharing Your Faith with a Muslim, Abdiyah Akbar Abdul-Haqq (Bethany House, 1992; ISBN 9780871235534)

Waging Peace on Islam, Christine Mallouhi (InterVarsity Press, 2002; ISBN 9780830823048)

■ Notes

What effect do the

Crusades have on

Muslim-Christian

relations today—and

how should we respond?

SCRIPTURE FOCUS	
	Numbers 14:18–23
	Nehemiah 9:1–4
	1 Corinthians 10:1–13
	1 John 1:8–9 and 2:1–2

THE CRUSADES—
A HAUNTING HISTORY

■

For some, the word *crusade* has positive connotations—it's an inspiring word, prompting believers to be courageous evangelists or to "fight" for a cause. For others, the word is brutal and hostile; it immediately brings to mind one of the darkest eras in Christian history—the Crusades. This centuries-long series of wars involving Western Christians, Eastern Christians, Jews, and Muslims is often cited as incontrovertible evidence of the danger of religious belief, but the Crusades were hardly a simple battle between tolerance and terrorism. Motives were mixed on all sides, and the signs of the times yielded confusing messages. In the *Christianity Today* article "Waging Peace on Islam," we'll hear from Warren Larson—a professor of Islam studies and former missionary to the Muslims—about the devastating and far-reaching effects this event of the distant past still has on Muslim-Christian relations today.

■ Before You Meet

Read "Waging Peace on Islam," an interview with Warren Larson by Stan Guthrie from *Christianity Today*.

WAGING PEACE ON ISLAM

A missionary veteran of Asia proposes one way to defuse Muslim anger about the Crusades.

An interview with Warren Larson by Stan Guthrie

The Crusades are long gone, but they are a live memory for Muslims today. Why? And how do Christians who minister to Muslims deal with this sad historical fact?

Warren Larson is director of the Zwemer Center for Muslim Studies at Columbia International University in Columbia, South Carolina. An associate professor of Islam with expertise in Muslim fundamentalism, the Canadian-born Larson was a church-planting missionary in the Punjab, Pakistan's largest province, from 1969 to 1991. (The small church he and his wife worked in remains active in the 99.9 percent Muslim city of Dera Ghazi Khan.) Today Larson travels widely in the Muslim world.

The First Crusade began nearly a millennium ago, and yet we often hear that Muslims think about those terrible events as if they happened yesterday. Why?

It's a perception of ongoing Western imperialism. There's a long history of unsuccessful encounters. The Crusades are in there, but also the fact that the Muslims were booted out of Spain in 1492. That's also very bitter for them. And then there was colonialism. Nine-tenths of the Muslim world was under colonialism. They connect all this—including Iraq, Iran, Afghanistan, and other things going on in the Middle East.

Why do so many Muslims continue to see the West as a Christian empire when, in fact, it's become highly secularized and pluralistic in recent decades?

One reason is that there are a lot of Christians here in the West. Muslims are convinced that evangelical Christians won the vote for George W. Bush and that America is quite Christian. Those perceptions, of course, are only partly true. One would hope [Muslims] would understand that the West is post-Christian, but in many ways, it hasn't quite hit them yet.

When we were living in Pakistan, they felt the things that went on in America—the immorality, the immodesty, the drinking—were sanctioned by Christianity.

Sometimes evangelicals in North America, particularly in the United States, say things that are not wise. They're not helping Muslim-Christian relations. In some cases, they have demonized Islam and denigrated the prophet [Muhammad]. They've done it publicly. This news travels far and wide, and Muslims print it in their newspapers. That keeps some of the feeling alive.

Can't we just explain to Muslims the concept of free speech and the open exchange of ideas?

Yes, but saying that Muhammad was a demonized pedophile doesn't seem accurate or fair. Nor is it wise. We have a free press, but we have to use it with discretion.

How do negative Muslim perceptions affect Christian missionaries and local Christians at street level?

In some areas of Pakistan, Islam has been radicalized, and anti-Americanism is higher today than when I was there. Partly as a result, the five hundred missionaries who were there have now been reduced to about one hundred.

Christians have suffered. There have been quite a few attacks in places such as Pakistan. Churches have been burned. Schools have been attacked. Muslim converts [to Christianity], in particular, have suffered and feel quite vulnerable. When I was in Ethiopia recently, the fellow who did my translating was a Somali. He was part of a group of believers, formerly Muslims, who came out of Somalia in 1994 when the U.S. military failed in Mogadishu. Islamists hunted down and killed fourteen members of his group. He got out of there by the skin of his teeth.

How should local Christians and missionaries respond to these historically negative associations with the Crusades in the minds of Muslims?

I think an apology is in order. But having said that, I think we have to hold Muslims accountable too. They might forget or not be aware that, starting in 1915, Turks killed more than a million and a half Armenian Christians. There have been unsuccessful encounters between Muslims and Christians for nearly the last 1,500 years, but [this history is] not all the fault of the West and Christians. Muslims have also done wrong.

Wouldn't you say that Christians have apologized because they recognized that they did not live up to the ideals of their faith, such as turning the other cheek? A lot of Muslims might think, however, that the Islamic doctrine of jihad justifies certain violent actions. Thus, they may not be so willing to apologize.

That's true. Islam doesn't teach you to forgive your enemies. But, for the sake of truth, we need to confront them. We can do it lovingly, but we need to do it.

When you forgive Muslims, they recognize the difference. They say, "We don't forgive anybody, but now we see that you're different." On November 20, 1979, when the holy Kaaba in Mecca was taken over by unnamed insurgents, we were living in Dera Ghazi Khan. The rumor went out, thanks to Ayatollah Khomeini, that it was the work of Americans and Jews. When the false rumor reached our city, a mob formed and attacked us at our house and burned our jeeps, burned our literature, smashed furniture, and could have killed us, but for the grace of God.

During this time, the American embassy was burned to the ground in Islamabad. A few days later, the news came out that [the perpetrators at the Kaaba were] not Americans and Jews, but Saudis. The police and the military in our city rescued us and grabbed a few of the rioters and put them in prison.

We went to them and said, "We forgive you. We're not going to lodge a case against you." Then, neighbors, some of the people who knew me well, embraced me.

They said, "Mr. Larson, we now know the difference between you and us. We do not forgive our enemies. When there's trouble between us, Sunnis and Shiites, we fight and burn one another's shops. But you have forgiven us."

That was a great help, because it furthered our cause.

I said, "We're just doing what Jesus taught us to do."

Do you see that as a model for future interactions?

I sure do. I think it's very much waging peace on Islam rather than taking a militant stance as Christians. It's a kind of spirit. It's doing mission in the light of the Cross, or in the shadow of the Cross. It's a spirit of reconciliation, and it certainly does help. And Muslims respond. They do.

Seeing Christ on the Cross forgive his enemies in *The Passion of the Christ* was really quite powerful for Muslims. They may have gone to see the movie with wrong motives, but the fact that he forgave his enemies from the Cross seemed to touch them. Many, many Muslims went to see this movie. It was very powerful.

Warren Larson is director of the Zwemer Center for Muslim Studies at Columbia International University, Columbia, South Carolina.

Stan Guthrie is managing editor, special projects for Christianity Today.

("Waging Peace on Islam" was originally published in full in *Christianity Today*, June 2005, Vol. 49, No. 6.)

For more insightful articles from *Christianity Today* magazine, visit http://www.ctlibrary.com/ and subscribe now.

■ Open Up

Select one of these activities to launch your discussion time.

Option 1

Discuss one of these icebreaker questions:

• Tell the group a little about your family history. Are there any funny or unique stories about your ancestors or memories you have of grandparents or great-grandparents? Where did your ancestors come from? What do you know about them?

• How do you feel about your family history? Good? Sentimental? Indifferent? Ashamed? Describe your thoughts.

• When you think of the history of the church, which people or events come to mind as positive aspects of Christian history? Why? On the flip side, which people or events come to mind for you as shameful aspects of Christian history? Explain.

Option 2

Create slips of paper with half of them reading "pro" and the other half reading "con." Then divide your group evenly into two teams by drawing papers and have a quick, on-the-spot debate. You *must* go on the team you drew, whether or not that represents your true opinion.

You'll discuss this issue:

Many Christian colleges and high schools have the "Crusader" as their mascot. Often the mascot is dressed in armor and holding a weapon, though just as often the friendly expression or cartoon appearance makes the Crusader seem innocuous enough. Should Christian groups use a Crusader as a mascot?

Pro: It is perfectly fine for Christians to use a Crusader as a school mascot. Many school mascots around the country hearken back to historical wars (Warriors, Trojans, Spartans, and so on)—that's just how it goes. Having a Crusader as a mascot does not imply that a school is endorsing negative aspects of a historical war. Mascots are meant to be fun and encourage school spirit; in most cases, the use of a Crusader is simply light-hearted and well-intentioned.

Con: The Crusader represents a sinful and embarrassing part of Christian history; it symbolizes actions and attitudes that are reprehensible and have no place in the Christian message. When others see a Crusader as a mascot—especially Muslims—they may not take it to be simply good-natured fun. On the contrary, they may feel insulted that Christians would treat the matter so light-heartedly. Christian schools should not have Crusaders as mascots because of the harm it can do to their witness in the larger community.

Run your quick debate by taking one minute to strategize, then two minutes for each team to present their case. Allow one minute per team to make a final rebuttal and conclusion.

■ The Issue

In 2000, Wheaton College changed their mascot from a Crusader to "Thunder." The change was initiated by students who felt a Crusader was a poor representation of what their school was really about. Wheaton College's President, Dr. Duane Litfin, said this about the change in a letter to Wheaton Alumni:

Throughout my education I covered the history of the Crusades several times. Yet my images of the Crusades remained fairly idealized. It was not until I became aware of how offensive the image of the Crusades is to large segments of the world that I was forced to take another look at these historical events, and what I discovered was anything but ideal. Christians massacring Muslims; Muslims massacring Christians; Western Christians killing Eastern Christians and vice versa. We are hard-pressed to find anything in these disastrous waves of fighting that our Lord might have approved.

- Do you agree with the reasoning of the Wheaton students and faculty in their decision to abandon the Crusader mascot? Why or why not?

- In what other ways does the history of the Crusades impact modern culture? Share examples from current events or from your personal relationships.

■ Reflect

Read Numbers 14:18–23; Nehemiah 9:1–4; 1 Corinthians 10:1–13; and 1 John 1:8–9 and 2:1–2 on your own. Take notes, jotting down your observations about the key issues or important phrases in the passages. What questions do they raise? What challenges do they present in regards to our relationship with the Muslim world?

■ Let's Explore

Before we discuss the Crusades and their impact on Muslim-Christian relations today, it's important to have a basic grasp on what the Crusades actually were. Read this short historical summary reaching from the Crusades to modern times:

The prophet Muhammad, drawing on a mixture of Christian, Jewish, and other sources, founded Islam in 610. Over the next four centuries, Islam expanded rapidly. Muslim armies pushed into Western Europe as far as modern France before being repelled by Charles Martel in 732. By 830 Muslims controlled some two-thirds of the ancient Christian world, including Spain, northern Africa, the Holy Land, and the Middle East. Within these territories, Christians and Jews had the option of converting to Islam or continuing their faiths under severe restrictions. Followers of other religions could convert to Islam or die.

The Crusades spanned the period of 1099 to 1291. Different campaigns had different objectives, but the main motivating factors were: (1) to regain control of the Holy Land, both for symbolic reasons and to ensure safe passage for Christian pilgrims visiting holy sites; (2) to rescue Eastern (Orthodox) Christians from Islamic oppression; (3) to gain spiritual benefits (such as reduced time in purgatory). Assorted economic, military, and political motives came into play as well, sometimes overwhelming spiritual aims. (A particularly tragic example of this occurred in 1204, when crusaders entangled in Venetian business interests attacked their Eastern Christian allies at Constantinople.) A few European Christians, such as St. Francis of Assisi, accompanied crusaders in hopes of preaching the gospel to the "infidels." At the end of the Crusades, which caused well over one million deaths and permanently split Eastern and Western Christendom, Muslims retained control of the Holy Land.

In 1300 Muslim Turks founded the Ottoman Empire in present-day Turkey. The Ottomans fought the Christian Byzantine Empire, taking its capital, Constantinople, in 1453. Ottomans challenged Christian rule in Western and Eastern Europe as well until the breakup of the empire following World War I. Western powers, who had begun colonial inroads in the 19th century, asserted their authority in the Middle East through much of the 20th century, achieving their most prominent intervention with the founding of Israel in 1948. The Islamic world seemed to be in decline until the Islamic Revolution in Iran in 1979 marked the ascendancy of a militant version of the religion.

The history of God's people is full of saints and sinners—and we can learn from all of them.

Read 1 Corinthians 10:1–13. Though most members of the church at Corinth were Gentiles, Paul admonished them with a lesson from Israel's history. He encouraged the Corinthians to identify with the ancient Jews (using the phrase "our ancestors") and emphasized the persistence of both human failings and God's faithfulness.

- Consider for a moment some of the worst aspects of the Crusades and try to imagine the real Christian people who participated in those acts. How does Paul's history lesson change your perspective on these far-from-perfect people?

- In his account of imprisonment under the Soviets, *Gulag Archipelago*, Russian Orthodox writer Aleksandr Solzhenitsyn wrote, "The line separating good and evil passes not through states, nor between classes, nor between political parties, either, but right through every human heart." Does this view of humanity strike you as biblical? Does it make you look at yourself differently? At your heroes? At your enemies?

- In 1 Corinthians 10, Paul used Israel's disobedience in the desert as the backdrop for a lesson on resisting temptation. What lessons can *we* draw from the story of the Crusades?

God's forgiveness does not free his people from all the consequences of past sins.

Sometimes God's people do terrible things, either because they misinterpret God's will, or because they simply fail to follow it. Ideally, they repent and make amends, but the story does not always end happily.

The Bible presents two strong messages about forgiveness that are sometimes hard for us to harmonize. On the one hand, God promises free and complete forgiveness of sin for those who seek it. Read 1 John 1:8–9 and 2:1–2. On the other hand, though, the Bible records many instances in which God's forgiveness does not wipe the slate clean in regards to the consequences of sin. Read one such example in Numbers 14:18–23. Though our spiritual forgiveness is total and complete, God doesn't always "clean up the mess" that results from our sin when it comes to human relationships or other earthly consequences.

- Can you think of other examples, from the Bible or your own life, in which sin's consequences lingered even after repentance?

- What do you see as the main lingering consequences of the Crusades? How do they affect Muslim-Christian relations in the big picture?

Though you may not realize it, the painful history of Christians and Muslims at war with each other may have a dramatic effect on your relationships with Muslim friends and co-workers. What to you might feel like the distant past may be a very real, painful, present wound for your Muslim friend.

- What do you think might be the best way to approach the issue of the Crusades in conversation with a Muslim? What might you say? How should you act?

"Waging Peace" with Muslims involves honestly acknowledging the wrongs of the past.

Nehemiah records the efforts of the exiles' return to Jerusalem and their efforts to rebuild the city's wall. In celebration of the wall's completion, Ezra calls God's people to commit to obeying God's Law. He then leads the people in celebrating an important holiday of worship—the Festival of Booths. Chapter 9 begins with another important gathering for God's people—a time of national confession and worship. Read Nehemiah 9:1–4. (The rest of the chapter contains the words of their remembrance, repentance, and worship.)

It's common in our culture to think of repentance and forgiveness as a personal thing—a way of dealing with one's own actions or relationships. But in this passage, God's people repent not only for wrongs they've committed, but also for the sins of their forefathers.

- Do you think this example applies to us today? Should *we* repent of sins we were not directly responsible for, such as actions of the church in the past or actions our nation has taken? Explain.

- Do you think we need to repent and seek forgiveness for the Crusades? If so, what might that look like? If not, why not?

In his interview with Stan Guthrie, Warren Larson described the way he thinks Christians should approach relationships with Muslims, saying, "I think it's very much waging peace on Islam rather than taking a militant stance as Christians. It's a kind of spirit. It's doing mission in the light of the Cross, or in the shadow of the Cross. It's a spirit of reconciliation, and it certainly does help."

"Waging peace" is a rather active phrase. Larson didn't say "feeling peaceful toward" or "avoiding conflict." Instead, like *waging* war, waging peace implies bold action.

- What does the phrase "waging peace" mean to you? In what ways does a "waging peace" mind-set differ from common attitudes toward Islam in the church today?

- How can we communicate a spirit of reconciliation with Muslims? What are some specific examples of how this can be done?

■ Going Forward

- When it comes to Christian-Muslim relations, do you think it is hard to forgive or to seek to be forgiven? Explain.

- In light of all you've discussed, do you feel hopeful, confused, or discouraged about Christian-Muslim relations in today's world? Why?

Though the Crusades took place hundreds of years ago, many Muslims still feel affronted, many Eastern Christians still feel betrayed, and many Jews still feel frightened at the prospect of Christian aggression. Christian attempts to apologize, including a "Reconciliation March" through Israel in 1999, seem to have accomplished little. (The Vatican has resisted calls from the Muslim world for a more formal apology.) As Christians, we have to believe that the gospel offers a way forward, but will likely continue to struggle to discern what that way is.

- Because Christians and Muslims have wronged each other greatly over the centuries, both sides have much to forgive and to be forgiven for. Christians (and Muslims) who regret actions taken in the name of their religion need to forgive some of their own people too. What might the first step in that forgiveness look like?

Pray as a group and consider the prayer in Nehemiah 9 as your model. As you pray together, recount some of God's miracles and blessings, name some of the wrongs done in the name of Christ throughout history and acknowledge their consequences, seek God's forgiveness and his healing, then praise and thank God for his guidance of his people throughout history.

■ Want to Explore More?

Recommended Resources

Christian History issue 40: The Crusades (www.christianhistorystore.com)

Christian History issue 74: Christians & Muslims (www.christianhistorystore. com)

Islam at the Crossroads: Understanding Its Beliefs, History, and Conflicts, P. Marshall, R. Green, and L. Gilbert (Baker, 2002; ISBN 0801064163)

Light in the Shadow of Jihad, Ravi Zacharias (Multnomah, 2002; ISBN 1576739899)

The Crusades: A Short History, Jonathan Riley-Smith (Yale, 1990; ISBN 0300047002)

Understanding Islam, James A. Beverley (Nelson Reference, 2001; ISBN 0785248978)

For primary documents, including Muslim accounts of the Crusades, see the Internet Islamic History Sourcebook, http://www.fordham.edu/halsall/islam/islamsbook.html.

■ Notes

How can the Bible's

teachings on peace and

violence help us sort

through the various

perspectives on violence

in Islam?

SCRIPTURE FOCUS

Matthew 5:9–12, 10:34–39, 11:12

IS ISLAM A
RELIGION OF PEACE?

■

The root of the word *Islam* is the Arabic word *salim*
which means "peace." In a speech in 2002, then
President George W. Bush declared, "Islam, as practiced
by the vast majority of people, is a peaceful religion, a
religion that respects others." Others have a drastically
different perspective, viewing Islam as anything but
peaceful. Regardless of our viewpoint, many of us find
it hard to reconcile the Qur'an's teachings on violence
and peace. But the Bible's teachings also reflect a similar
paradox. In this study, we'll look at attitudes toward peace
and violence in our own faith.

■ Before You Meet

Read "Is Islam a Religion of Peace?" by James A. Beverley from *Christianity Today* magazine. You may also want to review the appendix, "Islam 101," on p.172.

IS ISLAM A RELIGION OF PEACE?

The controversy reveals a struggle for the soul of Islam.

By James A. Beverley

Osama bin Laden, the world's most notorious terrorist, has handed Muslims everywhere their worst public-relations nightmare: September 11 as a picture, an embodiment, of Islam. Muslims now have to define themselves in relation to the day of infamy.

Abdulaziz Sachedina, a Muslim scholar at the University of Virginia, says he does not remember ever praying so earnestly that God would spare Muslims the blame for "such madness that was unleashed upon New York and Washington . . . I felt the pain and, perhaps for the first time in my entire life, I felt embarrassed at the thought that it could very well be my fellow Muslims who had committed this horrendous act of terrorism. How could these terrorists invoke God's mercifulness and compassion when they had, through their evil act, put to shame the entire history of this great religion and its culture of toleration?"

Every judgment about Islam, all reaction to Muslim doctrine, and each Muslim-Christian encounter are now cast in light of the events of that dreadful day.

Islam as a Path of Peace

There are three distinct interpretations of the events of September 11. The first view is that the terrorist acts do not represent Islam. President George W. Bush best expressed this notion when he said, "Islam is a religion of peace." One of the leading Muslims to echo this is Yusuf Islam (the former rock musician Cat Stevens, who now helps promote Muslim education in England). "Today, I am aghast at the horror of recent events and feel it a duty to speak out," he said in a London newspaper. "Not only did terrorists hijack planes and destroy life; they also hijacked the beautiful religion of Islam."

During an interfaith ceremony at Yankee Stadium on September 23, Imam Izak-El M. Pasha pleaded, "Do not allow the ignorance of people to have you attack your good neighbors. We are Muslims, but we are Americans. We Muslims, Americans, stand today with a heavy weight on our shoulders that those who would dare do such dastardly acts claim our faith. They are no believers in God at all."

Major Muslim organizations throughout North America, including the Council on American-Islamic Relations, the Islamic Society of North America, and the Muslim Students Association, denounced the work of the terrorists. The powerful American Muslim Council issued a press release on September 11, saying it "strongly condemns this morning's plane attacks on the World Trade Center and the Pentagon and expresses deep sorrow for Americans that were injured and killed. AMC sends out its condolences to all the families of the victims of this cowardly terrorist attack."

With the exception of Iraq, Muslim nations distanced themselves from the attack on America. "Iran has vehemently condemned the suicidal terrorist attacks in the United States," *Iran Today* reported in a front-page story on September 24, "and has expressed its deep sorrow and sympathy with the American nation." The governments of Bahrain, Egypt, Lebanon, Oman, Pakistan, Palestine, Qatar, Saudi Arabia, Turkey, United Arab Emirates, and Yemen expressed similar sentiments.

Leading intellectuals, who have argued that terrorist acts represent only fringe Muslims, have also promoted the view that Islam is a religion of peace. Edward Said, the controversial Columbia University professor, argued in *The Nation* that September 11 is an act of cultic religion. Comparing Islamists to the Branch Davidians and the Rev. Jim Jones, he said September 11 is a model of "the carefully planned and horrendous, pathologically motivated suicide attack and mass slaughter by a small group of deranged militants . . . the capture of big ideas by a tiny band of crazed fanatics for criminal purposes."

Mark Juergensmeyer, professor at the University of California at Santa Barbara and a specialist on religious violence, put it similarly: "Osama bin Laden is to Islam [what] Timothy McVeigh is to Christianity."

The Darker Side

After initial emphasis on Islam as a religion of peace, a second interpretation came to the fore. Editorials started to emerge that were less optimistic about Islam *per se* and far more alarmed about the scope and depth of militant Islam. Novelist Salman Rushdie, on whom the late Ayatollah Khomeini once issued a death order, wrote in *The New York Times*:

If this isn't about Islam, why the worldwide Muslim demonstrations in support of Osama bin Laden and Al Qaeda? Why did those ten thousand men armed with swords and axes mass on the Pakistan-Afghanistan frontier, answering some mullah's call to jihad? Why are the war's first British casualties three Muslim men who died fighting on the Taliban side? . . . [Islamists have] a loathing of modern society in general, riddled as it is with music, godlessness, and sex; and a more particularized loathing (and fear) of the prospect that their own immediate surroundings could be taken over—"Westoxicated"—by the liberal Western-style way of life.

Poverty is their great helper, and the fruit of their efforts is paranoia. This paranoid Islam, which blames outsiders, "infidels," for all the ills of Muslim societies, and whose proposed remedy is the closing of those societies to the rival project of modernity, is presently the fastest growing version of Islam in the world.

Others have been naming Islam's dark side as well, without suggesting that all Muslims are terrorists. Thomas Friedman, author of *From Beirut to Jerusalem*, has taunted Osama bin Laden in his *New York Times* columns, while also warning of the terrorist's popularity in Saudi Arabia, Pakistan, and other Muslim nations.

British journalist Julie Burchill wrote a scathing article in *The Guardian* against the "sustained effort on the part of the British media to present Islam—even after the Rushdie affair and now during the Taliban's reign of terror—as something essentially 'joyous' and 'vibrant,' sort of like Afro-Caribbean culture, only with fasting and *fatwas*."

Melanie Phillips, writing in *The Times of London*, raises the possibility of treason among British Muslims. "As if the progress of the Afghan war wasn't enough to worry about, a nightmare specter is emerging at home. The attitude of many British Muslims should cause the greatest possible alarm that we have a fifth column in our midst. . . . Thousands of alienated young Muslims, most of them born and bred here but who regard themselves as an army within, are waiting for an opportunity to help to destroy the society that sustains them. We now stare into the abyss, aghast."

In the weeks after the World Trade Center crumbled, there was no proof of an Islamic world totally united against terrorism. Rick Bragg reported in *The New York Times* about Muslim boys running through their school compounds in Pakistan on September 11. They were "celebrating, stabbing the fingers on one hand into the palm of the other, to simulate a plane stabbing into a building." Palestinian authorities went into overdrive to suppress images of youths celebrating the deaths in America.

September 11 as Islam

There is, finally, the view that September 11 represents authentic Islam, a notion adopted by Osama bin Laden and his many followers. His revolutionary zeal lacks no clarity. "The ruling to kill the Americans and their allies—civilians and military—is an individual duty for every Muslim who can do it in any country in which it is possible to do it," he said in February 1998. Muslim extremists from Bangladesh, Egypt, and Pakistan also signed this *fatwa*, titled "Urging Jihad Against Americans." Bin Laden told ABC News producer Rahimullah Yousafsai last winter that he would kill his own children, if it were necessary, to hit American targets.

Ironically, some Christian writers have also advanced the view that September 11 represents true Islam. Of these, the most influential is Robert A. Morey, the popular evangelical cult-watcher, who in recent years has targeted Islam as a deadly religion. Author of *The Islamic Invasion*, Morey has often debated leading Muslim apologists in fiery exchanges that have led to mob attacks on him and repeated calls for his death. Morey has accused Muhammad of being a racist, a murderer, an irrational zealot, and a pedophile. After September 11, Morey announced a spiritual crusade against Islam, and invited Christians to sign this pledge:

In response to the Muslim Holy War now being waged against us, We, the undersigned, following the example of the Christian Church since the 7th century, do commit ourselves, our wealth, and our families to join in a Holy Crusade to fight against Islam and its false god, false prophet, and false book. We, the undersigned, believe that Islam is the root of all Muslim terrorism, which is the fruit of Islam.

Christian scholars have criticized Morey for his invective, but he remains unmoved. He has argued that Muslims will start World War III. On his Web site, Morey invites Christians to fill in a "certificate of valor" that reads, "I wish to join in the Crusade of Christ against Islam. To that end, and to demonstrate in the crusade against Islam, I hereby donate toward emergency wartime funds."

The Rise of the Militants

Sorting through these three interpretations demands analysis of some deeper issues. First, we must come to grips with the vast unrest in the Islamic world, both now and over the last two centuries. There has been a growing radicalization in Islam since the early 1800s, both in response to the spread of Western colonialism and the demise of Muslim political supremacy.

Osama bin Laden traces his radicalism to the Wahhabism of his native Saudi Arabia, a movement that began with the reformer Muhammad ibn 'Abd al-Wahhab (1703–87), an advocate of a puritanical reading of Islamic law and belief. The Wahhabis threatened the interests of the Ottoman Turks and, in concert with the Saud dynasty, eventually gained control of Mecca and Medina, Islam's holiest cities.

A fundamentalist thrust in Islam emerged in Egypt as well, with the formation of the Muslim Brotherhood (also known as Al-Ikhwan al-Muslimun) in 1927. Tormented first by the presence of British rule and then by a tepid Muslim government, brotherhood founder Hassan al-Banna and Sayyid Qutb, his chief intellectual heir, sought by any means, including violence, to restore true Islamic rule to Egypt.

The brotherhood started branches in Jordan and Syria, and militant groups in India, Iran, and Iraq imitated its radicalism. Muhammad Nawab-Safavi started his Fedayeen-e-Islami movement in Iran in the 1930s and told his followers: "Throw away your beads and get a gun: for beads keep you silent whilst guns silence the enemies of Islam." Abul A'la Maududi organized his militant Jamaat-e-Islami in the Punjab in 1941. After the creation of Pakistan in 1947, Maududi tried repeatedly to convince the government to adopt his stricter version of Islamic rule.

Western awareness of militant Islam came with the radical overthrow of the Shah of Iran in 1979 and the establishment of harsh Shari'ah law under the Ayatollah Khomeini. American exposure to Islamic fundamentalism came with the arrest of Americans in Tehran, the bombing of the World Trade Center in 1993, the explosions at U.S. embassies in Africa, the attack on the USS Cole in Yemen, and then the horrors of September 11.

Interpreting Jihad

Every discussion of Islamic militancy turns eventually to two fundamental concerns. First, how much is Islamism (that practiced by fundamentalist Muslims open to violence) rooted in the teaching and practice of the prophet Muhammad? Would he celebrate the work of Osama bin Laden? Second, are the violent jihads of our day sanctioned by the Qur'an and by the actions of early Muslim leaders?

The prophet himself engaged in many military battles and could be merciless to his enemies, even those who simply attacked him verbally. His original sympathies with Jews and Christians as "Peoples of the Book" gave way to a harsher treatment when they did not follow Islam. In one infamous episode, Muhammad cut the heads off hundreds of Jewish males of the Beni Quraiza tribe who did not side with him in battle. The prophet is quoted as saying, "The sword is the key of heaven and hell; a drop of blood shed in the cause of Allah, a night spent in arms, is of more avail than two months of fasting or prayer: whosoever falls in battle, his sins are forgiven, and at the day of judgment his limbs shall be supplied by the wings of angels and cherubim."

In reference to the Qur'an, many have drawn attention to the famous passage in Surah 2:256: "Let there be no compulsion in religion." This verse fits well with other Qur'an verses in which jihad means personal and communal spiritual struggle or striving. But the Qur'an also uses jihad to mean "holy war," and the language can be extreme. Surah 5:33 reads, "The punishment of those who wage war against God and His Messenger, and strive with might and main for mischief through the land is: execution, or crucifixion, or cutting off of hands and feet from opposite sides, or exile from the land: that is their disgrace in this world, and a heavy punishment is theirs in the Hereafter."

Both the example of the prophet and some emphases in the Qur'an provided warrant for Islam's earliest leaders to spread Islam by military conquest. Bloody expansionism was also justified through original Islamic law that divided the world into two realms: Dar al-Harb (the land of war) and Dar al-Islam (land under Islamic rule). Both Paul Fregosi's *Jihad in the West* and Jewish scholar Bat Ye'or's *Decline of Eastern Christianity Under Islam* document the reality of Muslim crusades long before the notorious Christian crusades of the Middle Ages.

Out of the vortex of these realities emerge two different perspectives among modern Muslims. Islamists consider their actions a true jihad or "holy war" against infidels and the enemies of Islam. They believe it is right to target America, "the great Satan." Osama bin Laden believes that the Qur'an supports his campaign, that the prophet would bless his cause, and that Allah is on his side. But the vast majority of Muslims believe that nothing in Muhammad's life or in the Qur'an or Islamic law justifies terrorism.

Bernard Lewis, the great historian of Islam, noted in *The Wall Street Journal* that throughout history, Muslims have given jihad both spiritual and military meaning. Lewis also pays particular attention to the legal traditions in Islam about what constitutes just war. After noting the many limitations placed on military jihad, he writes, "What the classical jurists of Islam never remotely considered is the kind of unprovoked, unannounced mass slaughter of uninvolved civil populations that we saw in New York. For this there is no precedent and no authority in Islam."

"The Clash of Civilizations," Samuel Huntington's essay for Foreign Affairs (Summer 1993), has attracted considerable attention in recent months. Writing just after the Gulf War, Huntington analyzed the competing ideologies of our time and drew particular attention to the clash between Islam and the West. His concern has obvious merit, although critics have made a crucial point that Islam is no monolith. There are clashes within Islamic civilization itself.

What may emerge as the most significant factor in the current shape of our world, then, is not the clash between Islam and the West. It is, instead, the clash between Muslims as they try to define their faith for the 21st century. Islam clearly does not speak with one voice. It shows nearly as much diversity as does Christianity (see "A Many Splintered Thing"). The debate within Islam will be protracted, regardless of how long military campaigns continue against any Islamist movement.

Troubles in Palestine

The Palestinian question has also fueled the growth of Islamic militancy. Tensions in Palestine between Muslims and Jews date back to the first wave of Jewish immigrants in the late 1800s. The British government's 1917 Balfour Declaration heightened Arab unrest, as did the United Nations' support for a Jewish state thirty years later, leading to the formation of the State of Israel in May 1948.

Five wars between Arabs and Jews since Israel's formation create the context for modern Muslim-Jewish hostilities. These tensions increased with the rise of the first Intifadah ("uprising") in 1987, and a second Intifadah in 2000, following the breakdown of talks at Camp David between Yasser Arafat and Israeli Prime Minister Ehud Barak. Islamic militant groups like Hamas and Hizbollah call for an armed jihad against Israel. Many Palestinian Muslims celebrate the attack on America but also claim it was really the work of the CIA and Israel's Mossad.

In the mix of all this turmoil is the seemingly endless cycle of violence in Israel and Palestine. Here are just five examples of terrorist acts against Israelis in the year before September 11:

August 12—A suicide bombing at a café in Kiryat Motzkin wounded twenty-one.

August 9—A bombing at a pizza place in Jerusalem killed fifteen, including six children, and injured eighty.

June 1—A Palestinian suicide bomber associated with Hamas detonated an explosive belt that injured 120 and killed twenty at a nightclub in Tel Aviv.

May 9—Two fourteen-year-old Jewish boys were stoned to death at a cave near their small town of Tekoa, in the West Bank.

February 14—A Palestinian bus driver plowed into a crowd near Tel-Aviv, killing eight.

On the other hand, writers as diverse as Noam Chomsky, Hans Küng, Michael Lerner, Edward Said, and David Grossman (author of *The Yellow Wind*) argue for recognizing injustices done against Palestinians by Israel. They also argue for stronger American complaints against Israeli settlements in the West Bank and Gaza. In the last fifteen years, the case for a Palestinian state has grown more popular among moderate Jews and many analysts sympathetic to Israel.

"With or without Islamic fundamentalism, with or without Arab terrorism, there is no justification whatsoever for the lasting occupation and suppression of the Palestinian people by Israel," Amos Oz wrote in a *New York Times* editorial. "We have no right to deny Palestinians their natural right to self-determination. . . . Two huge oceans could not shelter America from terrorism; the occupation of the West Bank and Gaza by Israel has not made Israel secure—on the contrary, it makes our self-defense much harder and more complicated. The sooner this occupation ends, the better it will be for Palestinians and Israelis alike."

Human Rights Record

Beyond the issue of Palestine lies another concern. Is Islam fundamentally opposed to human rights by its inherently theocratic thrust? Why do Muslim countries have such deplorable records on human rights? Data made available by Freedom House, an organization that monitors political and civil rights in every country of the world, supports this assertion. Of the forty-one countries whose population is at least 70 percent Muslim, twenty-six are considered not free, and thirteen are partly free. Only two are free—meaning they protect political and civil rights as defined by the United Nations Declaration of Human Rights.

We can express the abuse of human rights in Muslim countries in other ways. Why is it that the government of Saudi Arabia welcomed Allied Forces to free Kuwait but forbids entry of non-Muslims to its country? Western governments allow Muslims to talk freely about their faith. Why can't Christians do the same in many Muslim countries? Muslims rightfully express concern about the denial of liberties to Palestinians. But are the rights of Jews protected in Indonesia? Are Hindus free in Pakistan?

Human beings are being traded as slaves in Sudan, a fact documented in Paul Marshall's *Their Blood Cries Out*. Has the government in Khartoum been flooded with protests from every corner of the Muslim world? Likewise, no one can deny the lack of women's rights under Islam, regardless of Muslim apologists' passion to the contrary. The widespread practice of female genital mutilation in Muslim countries alone signals the reality of women's oppression. Women are forbidden even to drive a car in Saudi Arabia.

Until they were freed suddenly in mid-November, eight expatriate Christians were on trial in Afghanistan on charges of Christian evangelism. Followers of Jesus in many Muslim countries can be put to death for sharing what they believe. It would be wonderful to know that the Muslim leaders who joined President Bush in public to express solidarity against Osama bin Laden were already on record as condemning the persecution of these Christians in Afghanistan. If not, why not?

In 1999 I had lunch with an American whose identity I must conceal lest I place his life in renewed danger. Over our meal, he told me of a simple but life-altering fact. A few years earlier, he realized that he no longer believed in Islam, and he abandoned his faith. As a result, he received death threats—not in Sudan, or Libya, or Iraq, but in the United States. Are American Muslim leaders disturbed that members of their communities threaten former Muslims with death? Do American Muslims long for adoption of Shari'ah law, which would mandate that Muslims who abandon their faith be put to death?

Rethinking Islam

Though many Muslims have tried to blame America and Israel for all the ills of the Muslim world, a rising number of Muslim intellectuals are calling for a new and radical self-criticism within Islam. This point has been articulated best by Kanan Makiya, author of *Republic of Fear* (on Saddam Hussein's Iraq) and *Cruelty and Silence* (a powerful protest against the timidity of Arab intellectuals to address the dark side of the militant Islamic Middle East).

Makiya writes in a *London Observer* article, "Fighting Islam's Ku Klux Klan":

Arabs and Muslims need today to face up to the fact that their resentment at America has long since become unmoored from any rational underpinnings it might once have had; like the anti-Semitism of the inter-war years, it is today steeped in deeply embedded conspiratorial patterns of thought rooted in profound ignorance of how a society and a polity like the United States, much less Israel, functions.

His article ends with these words:

Muslims and Arabs have to be on the front lines of a new kind of war, one that is worth waging for their own salvation and in their own souls. And that, as good out-of-fashion Muslim scholars will tell you, is the true meaning of jihad, a meaning that has been hijacked by terrorists and suicide bombers and all those who applaud or find excuses for them. To exorcise what they have done in our name is the civilizational challenge of the twenty-first century for every Arab and Muslim in the world today.

The events of September 11 have led some non-Muslims to reconsider their rhetoric against the United States and Israel. Of most significance, here is the Australian activist, Helen Darville, author of *The Hand that Signed the Paper*. She writes:

I have watched, since that day, the cozy leftist pieties of my youth disintegrate. Those pieties will be familiar to many of you. Chief among them is the old saw that in order to understand horrors, one must be willing to contextualize them. And if that mitigates them, so be it.

The images of Palestinians cheering as planes carved into skyscrapers made me sick at heart. One fat woman in ugly specs will stay with me for a long time. Don't go there, I chanted under my breath as she ululated with joy. Don't go there. That's where the Nazis went, and in that way lies madness. There are accounts beyond number of Eastern European peasants cheering German executioners on, trying to pry the carbines from their hands: let me shoot them, Herr Soldat.

A lot of these peasants were raised in the church. Christian anti-Semitism has a long and terrible history, as does Christian aggression against Islam during the Crusades and against fellow Christians during the Wars of Religion. But after each outpouring of violence, the church has been forced to ask itself: Is this what Christianity is about? Is this what Christ came for? Is this how we want to live in his name?

In time the answers came, and except for small, radical fringes, Christianity as a whole has repudiated war, coercion, and hate as ways to further the Christian message.

Islam stands at such a crossroads since September 11. The tensions it has been facing for centuries have risen to the surface. Is Islam a religion of peace? Does it believe in human rights? Can it find a way to be a part of the human community without violently insisting on its own way?

We hear so many differing accounts of Islam today precisely because Muslims are in the midst of a struggle for the soul of Islam. We would be wise as Christians, humbled by our own past, to remember that as we seek to understand and engage Muslims today out of love for Christ.

James A. Beverley is professor of theology and ethics at Tyndale Seminary in Toronto; He is author of *Understanding Islam* (Thomas Nelson).

("Is Islam a Religion of Peace?" was originally published in *Christianity Today*, January 7, 2002, Vol. 46, No. 1, Page 32.)

For more insightful articles from *Christianity Today* magazine, visit http://www.ctlibrary.com/ and subscribe now.

■ Open Up

Select one of these activities to launch your discussion time.

Option 1

Discuss one of these icebreaker questions:

• How do you personally feel about violence? What are situations in which you feel use of violence is appropriate? Or, if you are a pacifist, explain your view.

• What adjectives come to mind when you think of Islam? Is violence prominent in your understanding of Islam? Explain.

• How do you generally feel about violence in the Bible, such as wars and murders portrayed in the Old Testament or martyrdom described in the New Testament? Do these accounts bother you—or do you feel comfortable with them? Why?

Option 2

Discuss these case studies (both based on true stories):

Case Study 1

Imagine you're a pastor of a church. A twelve-year-old girl named Khoula begins attending services. She comes with a young friend from school who has talked openly about her Christian faith. In time you learn that Khoula is from a Muslim family. Her father works for a company based in Saudi Arabia, and the family will be in the United States for at least three years while he attends graduate school.

Khoula attends Sunday school and worship services for several weeks. Her parents have allowed this so Khoula can deepen her friendship with the girls she attends with. Eventually, Khoula expresses an interest in knowing more about faith in Jesus Christ. She prays to receive Christ and wants to be baptized. What do you do?

Later you learn that Khoula's father, whose practice of Islam appears to be nominal, does not object to her church attendance and even her baptism. He sees it all as part of their "American experience." Her mother, however, a strict adherent to Islam, objects strenuously.

As the war on terror continues to dominate the news, your relationship with the family grows more and more strained. They seem to resent your "influence" on their daughter; you find yourself harboring bitterness toward them and ambivalence about their religion.

- The child begs to be baptized and to join the church. You know, though, that this will cause serious conflict between the child and her mother—and between yourself and her parents. What do you do?

- Should you continue to reach out to them? If so, how?

Case Study 2

Now imagine a conversation with Ashraf, a young man from a militant Muslim family in the Middle East. He converted to Christianity several years ago but has kept it a complete secret. Now, studying as a college student in the States, he finally feels more free to express his faith. Ashraf has begun to feel like he should tell his family about his conversion when he returns home for the summer. Ashraf wants to be honest about his beliefs, but he is certain that his family will completely disown him. He fears, too, that extended family members will try to kill him. You know, from what he's told you about his family, that his fears are well-founded.

- What would you advise him to do? Why?

■ The Issue

In his article, James A. Beverly highlights three views on violence in Islam.

The first is that Islam is essentially a peaceful religion; those who practice violence in the name of Islam are outside the scope of the Qur'an's teachings. He notes professor Mark Jurgensmeyer's succinct summary of this viewpoint: "Osama bin Laden is to Islam [what] Timothy McVeigh is to Christianity."

The second perspective acknowledges the peaceful aspects of Islam while also drawing attention to its "darker side." Beverley notes the observations of Salman Rushdie, who drew attention to violent demonstrations and abhorrent killings, saying, "This paranoid Islam, which blames outsiders, 'infidels,' for all the ills of Muslim societies, and whose proposed remedy is the closing of those societies to the rival project of modernity, is presently the fastest growing version of Islam in the world."

The final view is that the terrorism of September 11th and other subsequent acts of extreme violence are representative of the core beliefs of Islam. Beverley draws attention to the assertions of Robert A. Morey who "has accused Muhammad of being a racist, a murderer, an irrational zealot, and a pedophile." Further, Morey has called Christians to sign a statement that declares, in part, "We, the undersigned, believe that Islam is the root of all Muslim terrorism, which is the fruit of Islam."

- When have you encountered these varying perspectives? Share an example.

- Which perspective best represents your own view of Islam? Or how does your viewpoint differ from those Beverley summarized?

The concluding four paragraphs in James Beverley's article turn the issue from peace and violence among adherents of Islam to peace and violence within Christianity. He says Christianity has "repudiated war, coercion, and hate as ways to further the Christian message." Yet the Old

Testament contains multiple examples in which acts of war and violence were done in God's name—often in obedience to his direct commands. In this study we'll examine the varying perspectives the Bible offers on the subject of peace and violence.

■ Reflect

Take a few moments to read 1 Samuel 17:45–54 and Joshua 6:16–21; then read Jesus's words in Matthew 5:9–12; 10:12–14, 21–22, 33–39. Write down what stands out to you most about the language in these passages. Which statements stand out to you most? What similarities or apparent contradictions do you observe between these passages? What questions do they raise for you?

■ Let's Explore

The story of God's people is far from peaceful.

• Who are your favorite Old Testament heroes or what are your favorite Old Testament stories? Why? How many of them include acts of violence?

Some of the most memorable stories from children's Sunday school tell about the great heroes of the Bible and their military conquests. Understandably, the stories are usually sanitized a bit to make them appropriate for children; they're even portrayed by jovial singing and dancing pickles, asparagus, and tomatoes in the popular VeggieTales series.

For many of us, the clear-cut, good-guy versus bad-guy scenario from Mrs. Thompson's Sunday school class is much more preferable—and easier to grasp—than the brutal reality of these biblical accounts. The Old

Testament's portrayal of Israel's wars is certainly not sanitized! It recounts thousands upon thousands of deaths in battles against pagan nations and depicts horrific acts of violence. You probably didn't learn about Jael's heroic assassination of an enemy leader by driving a tent peg through his temple (in Judges 4:21) or David carrying Goliath's severed head all the way back to Jerusalem (1 Samuel 17:54) as a child! Perhaps the most shocking to our modern sensibilities, though, is God's direct endorsement or overt involvement in many of these acts of violence.

Re-read these verses from two favorite Old Testament stories: David's confrontation with Goliath in 1 Samuel 17:45–54 and Joshua's battle for Jericho in Joshua 6:16–21.

- What's your gut reaction to these passages? to Joshua 6:21? Explain.

Today, movies and television shows depicting acts of Muslim terrorism take a cue from reality, showing suicide bombers and terrorists shouting "Allahu akbar!" ("God is great!") before they blow themselves up or commit some other act of violence. This cry—*Allahu akbar*—is a phrase real-life jihadists use as a rallying cry and as a justification for their actions.

It may be difficult to imagine groups of devoted Christians today shouting "God is great!" or "In Jesus's name!" before committing an act of violence (though there may be some extremists who think this way). Yet there are several examples in the Old Testament that bear striking similarities to this cry; David, Joshua, and countless other warriors and leaders in the Old Testament declared and firmly believed that they battled in God's name, for God's sake, and with God's endorsement. Often gatherings of worship and prayer took place directly after a battle—even amidst the surroundings of burned homes and dead people and animals.

- How are the acts of violence done in God's name in the Old Testament (like David saying "I come to you in the name of the LORD All-Powerful" in 1 Samuel 17:45) like or unlike acts of violence done in the name of Allah today?

Some struggle to integrate the "God of war" images in the Old Testament with the teachings of the "Prince of Peace" in the New Testament. It can be a challenge to understand and accept both the violent or wrathful aspects of God's character alongside Christ's example of peacemaking.

- Has this been a struggle for you? How do you incorporate the two? How might you explain these paradoxical aspects of biblical teaching to a friend who is struggling to understand them?

Jesus's teachings were not entirely *peaceful.*

Matthew 10 contains the marching orders Jesus gave his disciples before sending them to minister in his name. His troop includes Simon the Zealot. It is not his zeal for the Lord that earns Simon that title. Zealots were members of a resistance movement that advocated the overthrow of the Roman government. They were credited with knifings of government leaders. They would slip in and out of crowds in public places, often sliding short blades between the ribs of enemies. These were violent times, and these were violent men. Simon had been one of them.

- How do you imagine Jesus' statement in Matthew 10:34 sat with Simon the Zealot? How do *you* react to these words? Why?

In commissioning the disciples for their short-term mission trip, Jesus gave them power to heal and perform miracles, and he gave them instructions. His words on such a simple theme as greeting and departure are helpful.

Review Matthew 10:12–14. The greeting here is the Hebrew word *Shalom*, meaning peace. *Shalom* can be used at first meeting or departure, or as a blessing. But Jesus issues a caution. The peace greeting/blessing is not to be spread indiscriminately.

- Sometimes we feel that as Christians we always have to be "nice" or that we must always avoid rocking the boat. But Matthew 10:12–14 implies otherwise. When, if ever, do you think it's appropriate for Christians to do or say things that aren't "nice" or "peaceful"? Share examples from your own life.

In Matthew 10:35, Jesus declares one arena for his swordplay: family relationships. He quotes Micah 7:6 in saying his message will turn family members against each other. In Matthew 10:21–22 and 32–33, Jesus also speaks in strong terms. His teachings here are set against the backdrop of eternity, and they have eternal consequences. These are ominous predictions. The language Jesus uses makes it seem that Christians are at war.

- Do you think Jesus's talk of violence is a hyperbole, or should it be taken literally? Where do you see evidence of such "violence"?

We should consider for a moment the personal motivation involved in the use of violence for religious advancement. Consider, for example, the motivations of Muslim suicide bombers or hijackers. Their deaths were, in their own view, a noble sacrifice that earned them divine favor. These men took literally the words attributed to Muhammad: "The sword is the key of heaven and hell; a drop of blood shed in the cause of Allah, a night spent in arms, is of more avail than two months of fasting or prayer: whosoever falls in battle, his sins are forgiven, and at the day of judgment his limbs shall be supplied by the wings of angels and cherubim."

- Review Matthew 10:39. Can you think of examples where Christians literally lost their lives in the cause of Christ? What's the difference between such sacrifice and the actions of suicide bombers?

Sometimes Jesus sounds as if he wanted all his followers to become pacifists.

The Messiah was predicted to be a "Prince of Peace" (Isaiah 9:6). Some of his listeners—certainly Simon the Zealot would have cheered Jesus's war-like language to describe the advance of his kingdom. They wanted a conquering *Prince* of Peace.

Only now, two thousand years later, and a thousand years after the Crusades, do these verses seem so incongruous with the fair-haired Jesus of the Renaissance paintings. We generally think of Jesus as the Prince of *Peace*. His public sermons and private conversations certainly advocated peace: "Blessed are the peacemakers"; "I give you peace, not as the world gives"; "Turn the other cheek"; and "Go the second mile." And there's the admonition to pray for our enemies.

Re-read Matthew 5:9–12.

Christianity has wrestled with this one for centuries. Even now, believers know the need to pray for our enemies, to forgive our attackers, and at the same time to support our government's God-given authority to exact justice (Romans 13:4). In our time, we once again have the responsibility to reconcile these teachings. The question is, how?

- Does Jesus's teaching in Matthew 10:34 conflict with Matthew 5:9? How do you reconcile them?

- Jesus's words here are not mere sentiments—they are meant to be taken very seriously. How do they personally challenge you? In what situations do you feel God may be calling you to be a peacemaker in a radical way?

■ Going Forward

On September 13, 2001, two days after the horrific September 11 terrorist attacks, Reshma Memon Yaqub—a Muslim American—wrote this in the *Washington Post*:

Like every American, I am afraid . . . Like every American, I am outraged. And I want justice. But perhaps unlike many other Americans, I'm feeling something else too. A different kind of fear. I'm feeling what my six million fellow American Muslims are feeling—the fear that we too will be considered guilty in the eyes of America, if it turns out that the madmen behind this terrorism were Muslim. . . . I was briefly heartened to hear author Tom Clancy, interviewed on CNN, explaining that Islam is a peaceful religion and that we as Americans must not let go of our ideals of religious tolerance, because it's the way our country behaves when it's been hurt that really reflects who we are. Still, I'm afraid that Americans might view the televised images of a few misguided and deeply wounded people overseas celebrating the pain that America is now feeling, and will assume that I too must share that anti-American sentiment, that I, or my family, or my community, or my religion, could be part of the problem. . . . . In fact, Islam forbids such acts of violence.

- What might you say if you were having a conversation with Yaqub? How would you explain your view of Islam, or your view of her as an American Muslim?

- Which of the following would you say should be the Christian's goal in relation to Muslims worldwide: tolerance, understanding, peaceful coexistence, conversion, or war? Alternately, which should be the Christian's goal in relation to Muslims on a personal level, such as with friends, neighbors, or co-workers?

Form pairs to discuss this final question:

- How do you feel God challenging you to more intentionally live as a peacemaker? You may share ideas related to your relationships with Muslims or you may feel challenged in other avenues of peacemaking such as in personal family relationships or through political action.

Pray in pairs, asking God for discernment about living as peacemakers. Also, pray by name for Muslims you know.

■ Want to Explore More?

Recommended Resources

Books presenting Islam as a primarily violent religion:

Religion of Peace?: Islam's War Against the World, Gregory M. Davis (World Ahead Publishing, 2006; ISBN: 097789844X)

Religion of Peace?: Why Christianity Is and Islam Isn't, Robert Spencer (Regnery Publishing, 2007; ISBN: 1596985151)

Books presenting Islam as a primarily peaceful religion:

Islam, Peace, and Tolerance, Zahid Aziz (Ahmadiyya Anjuman Lahore Publications, U.K., 2007; ISBN: 1906109001)

War, Peace and Non-Violence, Imam Muhammad Shirazi (Tahrike Tarsile Qur'an, 2001; ISBN: 1879402831)

How does Jesus's

fulfillment of the Old

Testament Law distinguish

it from Islamic Law?

SCRIPTURE FOCUS

Matthew 5:17–18

Galatians 3:19–29

LAW VERSUS GRACE

■

Recently there have been international news stories regarding the stoning of women and girls in the Muslim world who are accused of crimes like immodesty or adultery. It can be shocking for westerners to open their morning paper, hot cup of coffee in hand, only to find a horrific story about this inhumane and unjust treatment. It may be easy to feel outraged and think, "Only the Islamic religion could sanction such barbaric behavior!"

Ironically, the early practice of Old Testament law doesn't veer far from some of these news stories and we can easily find ourselves holding an apparent double standard. How should we react to the modern day practice of Islamic stoning, for example, while also acknowledging that stoning was practiced in ancient Israel? Drawing from "Islam's Uncertain Future," an interview with Paul Marshall, this study will explore the similarities and differences between Old Testament law and *Shari'ah* (strict Islamic law). Further, this discussion will point to the hope that Jesus brings as the fulfillment of the law.

■ Before You Meet

Read "Islam's Uncertain Future," an interview of Paul Marshall by Stan Guthrie from *Christianity Today*. You may also want to review the appendix, "Islam 101," on p.172.

ISLAM'S UNCERTAIN FUTURE

Freedom House's Paul Marshall says Shari'ah is both less and more dangerous than you think.

Interview by Stan Guthrie

Paul Marshall is a senior fellow at the Hudson Institute's Center for Religious Freedom and the editor of *Radical Islam's Rules: The Worldwide Spread of Extreme Shari'a Law* (Rowman & Littlefield Publishers, 2005). He is interviewed here by Stan Guthrie, a CT senior associate editor and author of *Missions in the Third Millennium: 21 Key Trends for the 21st Century*.

You distinguish between two kinds of Shari'ah, or Islamic law, as understood and implemented by Muslims worldwide. What are they?

In the last three years, I've been to various parts of the Muslim world talking to people about Shari'ah. I use the term *extreme Shari'ah* for the sorts of things that happen in Saudi Arabia, Iran, or Pakistan—people getting accused of blasphemy or stoned for adultery, and so on. But most Muslims use the term in a very broad sense. In Indonesia, if you ask people, "Do you think women should be stoned to death for adultery?" more than 80 percent of the population says no. If you ask, "Is it okay for Indonesia to have a woman leader?" more than 90 percent of the population says yes, that's fine. So they have something very different in mind from the Taliban. You get similar results right now in Iraq. [When asked,] "Do you think Iraq should be governed by Islamic law?" about 80 percent say yes. If you ask, "Do you think there should be legal equality between men and women?" about 80 percent say yes.

For many Muslims, the term *Shari'ah* has a very broad sense that the country should be governed in a way that God wants.

So most Muslims would not agree that, say, the punishment for theft should be amputation of one's hand?

Correct. They see that as something that used to be done, but not really fitting for the sorts of societies we live in now, that it's not the core of what Islam is about.

Does this attitude point to modernizing tendencies in Islam?

There are modernizing tendencies, but [a larger factor is that] the vast majority of Muslims in the world live in Africa and Asia, not in the Middle East. Their views on Islam are not very precise. They don't read the Qur'an; they can't read it.

Does that present an opportunity for extreme Islamists to clarify the Qur'an for them in a way that would be dangerous for heretics and adulterers?

Very much so. In countries such as Bangladesh or Indonesia, Islam historically has been very broad and moderate in outlook. But radical Islamic preachers, especially from the Gulf, especially funded by Saudi Arabia, are coming in. They've built mosques. They're providing people, imams, scholarships. And so you're getting an increasing radicalization in these populations that beforehand were more or less theologically illiterate. People are telling them, "If you want to be a true Muslim, a good Muslim, a proper Muslim, this is what you should do." This means, essentially, that they should start imitating Saudis.

How did extreme Shari'ah spread across the world?

In 1975, only one major country practiced these types of laws: Saudi Arabia. Beginning in 1979, you had the overthrow in Iran of the Shah by Ayatollah Khomeini, and Iran began to institute similar laws. There are differences: Iran is Shiite; Saudi Arabia is Sunni. But in terms of the *hudud* laws, the criminal laws, which involve amputation, crucifixion, stoning, and so on, they're very similar in outlook. In both cases, the status of women is very, very poor. The status of minorities is very, very poor.

Within Pakistan, the growth of such laws has been gradual. Through the 1980s, [we've seen] the increased influence of Shari'ah law, especially under General [Muhammad] Zia-ul-Haq, and the introduction of blasphemy laws for anybody insulting God, the Qur'an, or the Prophet Muhammad.

Beginning in 1983 in Sudan, the National Islamic Front, an offshoot of the Muslim Brotherhood in Egypt, came into power. It instituted an extremely draconian form of Shari'ah. It executed people who opposed these laws on the grounds that opposing its type of Shari'ah was itself against Shari'ah. That was one of the factors that precipitated the civil war between the largely Arab, Muslim northern Sudan and the largely black, African Christian south. In Chechnya, southern Russia, rebels have been trying to imitate the Sudanese legal code.

How did it come to Nigeria?

Beginning in 1995, the state of Zamfara began to institute these types of laws. Of thirty-six states in the country, twelve of them now have these types of laws on the books. Some are much more severe than others. But essentially this has happened right across the northern swath of Nigeria, and there's increased pressure in the central areas of Nigeria.

In nearly all of these countries [Iran, Pakistan, Sudan, and Nigeria], some form of Islamic law had been operating already . . . laws governing marriage, divorce, inheritance, and family law. But when I talk about the spread of Shari'ah, I mean that they changed the criminal code. They changed the law of evidence within the courts so that evidence from men and women was given different weight. They segregated public transportation systems so that unmarried men and women could not travel together, and so on. It's a quantum leap in the expression of Islam.

Has this extreme form of Islam spread elsewhere?

No other countries have adopted it wholesale. In fact, Malaysia has resisted these types of Shari'ah. In the last ten years, the two northern states tried to institute these laws. Because Malaysia is a federation, the federal government has the power to strike down these laws, and it has. But still, people in those two states have been arrested for blasphemy. Even though [such treatment] is strictly illegal, [local] governments can usually find a way to put someone in prison. Similarly, in Indonesia, there has been strong resistance at the national level to these types of laws. But at a town level or a county level, more extreme groups are starting to implement the laws. Indonesia is a big, sprawling country, and in lots of pockets around the country, people carry out the laws in their own way. You get vigilantes operating. In parts of western Java, someone driving a car on a Friday afternoon, Muslim or Christian, may get [his or her] car stoned.

You'll also find this going on in Bangladesh. It's not the government doing this, but if you're in poor, remote areas, you'll often find yourself subject to these laws.

What has been the impetus to spread extreme Shari'ah over the last thirty years?

In many of these countries, economically they have not been doing well. There's also extremely widespread corruption. Islamist parties, when they have campaigned, have spoken of poverty. They've also pointed out, correctly, the tremendous corruption. They've said, "The reason for our poverty, the reason our country is not doing well, is that we are not good Muslims. If we were truly faithful, if we were strict Muslims, we would do much better." They also say, "We're very committed Muslims. We will not be corrupt." And a lot of the support for more extreme forms of Islam comes from people who think, *While they may be much too strict for me, at least they're going to be honest. I won't have to pay a bribe for every single thing I need in life.*

Another reason is, again, the export of Muslim missionaries and literature from Saudi Arabia and Iran.

What percentage of the Muslim world supports extreme Shari'ah?

The percentages are very hard to come by. In Indonesia, people who support more radical Islamist parties make up about 13 percent or 14 percent of the population. Back in 1983, the National Islamic Front received about 12 percent of the vote in Sudan. In Pakistan, the numbers are similar. In Nigeria, support has been much higher, but mainly, I think, because of anti-corruption motivations. You're probably looking worldwide at 10 percent to 15 percent of the population.

Would that include support for Al Qaeda?

Not necessarily. Certainly, some of those people would. Perhaps 10 percent or 15 percent—that's a broad estimate, a guess—want to institute the type of society that Al Qaeda wants. Think of the Taliban. Think of Iran. Think of Saudi Arabia. Many of them push for that peacefully. The 10 percent or 15 percent are people who share the goal, but not the means. They may applaud Al Qaeda. If you ask them if they like [Osama] bin Laden, very often the answer is yes. He's widely admired. If you say, "Do you support the killing of prisoners by Zarqawi in Iraq?" they'll say no. And they might add there's no evidence that Al Qaeda does those things. So there's broad sympathy. The number who would actively engage in and give money to such movements would be a couple of percent.

What is the ultimate goal of the Islamists?

There are four points. One is to unite Muslims, who are fragmented into different countries and faiths, as one political unit. Two is that they will be governed by a caliph—one political and religious ruler of the united Muslim world. Three, the area controlled by Muslims will be ruled by forms of extreme Shari'ah law. A fourth point, which certainly the terrorists share with some others, is that the reunited Muslim political grouping would organize to wage war, *jihad*, against the rest of the world to continue the expansion of Islam until it has conquered the whole world.

But while all would like to export it, not all believe in trying to spread it by war. For the moment, they just want to control their own area, the places where they live, and try to make sure it's the form of Islam they feel is right.

Is Islam a religion of peace?

Islam was often warlike in its first centuries. Islamic rule was spread by military conquests, so it's certainly not true that Islam is a religion of peace in the same way that Quakers or the Amish is a religion of peace. Conflict and war go back a long way in Islamic history. But I wouldn't say that war is a necessary feature of Islam, that whenever you have Islam, you're going to have war. Islam has often been a warlike religion. That does not mean it has to be a warlike religion now.

Is militant Islam the real Islam?

I speak of existing Islam. That is, what is Islam like now, what are Muslims like now. I'm not in a position to say what authentic Islam is.

I will say that if you go through the Bible, you will also find the death penalty for idolatry. You'll find draconian punishments for adultery. You will find war in the name of God. I know of almost no Christians, even the most conservative, who believe that it's necessary to do those things in order to be a true Christian. We need to be careful not to have a double standard. There are certain things within Christianity, within Judaism, that were for a particular time. We need to allow Muslims to say the same thing.

Is extremist Islam growing in Europe and North America?

Certainly in Europe. One of the frightening things about Europe is that the second- and third-generation immigrants are much more radical than their parents. You're not getting assimilation; you're getting the opposite. In places such as England, the first generation of immigrants from Pakistan thirty or forty years ago came in, got menial jobs, opened shops, and were sort of marginalized but relatively peaceful. They wanted to make a success of life. The radicals are their children and in some cases even their grandchildren. As time goes on in Europe, the Muslim populations are becoming more radical, and, of course, the total numbers of Muslims are increasing. This is a frightening phenomenon for Europeans.

In the United States, the sociology of the Muslim population is very, very different. In Europe, many Muslim immigrants are low income, very poor, brought in to do menial jobs. In some ways within the society, they fill the slot that illegal immigrants fill in the United States. But in the United States, our Muslim population tends to be highly educated. I think more than 60 percent have degrees, and, in general, they do not live in separate neighborhoods. Whether radicalism is growing, I don't know. There are indications it is among African Americans and in prison populations.

Are Islam and democracy compatible?

Yes, they are. Indonesia and Turkey are among the largest Muslim populations in the world. They've got great problems. Often their elections have not been that clean. But they are functioning democracies. Mali in Africa is a very poor country, 99 percent Muslim. It's very free and has free and fair elections. Islam and democracy, as a practical matter, do coexist in the world. The big problem tends to be in the Arab world. Democracies are very hard to come by [there].

How does extreme Shari'ah affect Christians when Islamists gain control?

Almost immediately, there are restrictions on the building or repair of churches or the expansion of Christianity. You must stay where you are; you must stay in a subordinate position. Second, churches built without permits get destroyed. Third, Christians are often accused of blasphemy against Islam or of criticizing Islam. The pressure becomes very bad indeed. You get a community that is isolated and marginalized. Preaching the gospel to a Muslim is very strongly forbidden. That can get you killed. Or, if a Muslim decides to convert to Christianity or, indeed, to any other religion, there's a good chance that he or she will be killed as an apostate.

How should Christians under such pressure respond?

It will depend on the situation. If you're in a situation of severe threat, such as in Iran or Afghanistan, you keep your head down and simply manage the best you can. In situations where there are greater possibilities for change, such as Pakistan or Egypt, the Christian community becomes more outspoken. In Nigeria, there has been violent resistance by Christian bodies. Much of the violence consists of attacks by Muslims on Christians, but there are attacks the other way around as well. Then you have Sudan, in which—partly because of Shari'ah—the Christians and others have waged war to resist control by radical Islam. You see quite a range of options going on, and which one is right will very much depend on the circumstances. You have to make a judgment on what is possible.

So is taking up arms sometimes justifiable for Christians in your view?

Oh, yes, very much so. The Armenians have a long history of doing that, also the Ethiopians. These are areas where Christians still control territories and have often fought to maintain them. The defense through arms of a community and territory may well be a legitimate option, and that was the case in southern Sudan. The government was, in fact, waging a genocidal war, and the result could very likely have been the extermination of the Christian community. That's happened in many other places, such as Central Asia. I think on just-war grounds that can certainly be defended.

What should Western Christians do?

Develop strong relations with the Christian communities in those areas and find out what they need. Also, cultivate relations with Muslims in those countries and elsewhere to raise these questions. But remember that it's much more important for Muslims and Christians to talk locally. Muslims in the Middle East should talk to Christians in the Middle East.

As you look at the spread of extreme Shari'ah law and some of the tensions within Islam, are you hopeful or pessimistic?

If we're talking about the next few decades, I'm pessimistic. The influence of extreme forms of Islam and Shari'ah appear to be growing. Radical sentiment as a whole seems to be on the increase in the Muslim world. It's still a minority, but the people pushing for it are committed, organized, well funded, and have clear goals. The people who are opposed to them are often not well funded, organized, or committed, and they don't have a clear goal. When you have small, committed groups and a fairly amorphous majority group, the small, committed groups can make headway. I see that happening around the world. Regarding the struggle against radical Islam, to the degree that it's a war of ideas, it's a war that so far the radicals are winning.

Paul Marshall is the author and editor of over twenty books on religion and politics, especially religious freedom, including more recently, Radical Islam's Rules: the Worldwide Spread of Extreme Sharia Law *and* Religious Freedom in the World.

Stan Guthrie, author of Missions in the Third Millennium: 21 Key Trends for the 21st Century *is managing editor of special projects for* Christianity Today.

("Islam's Uncertain Future" was originally published in *Christianity Today* in February 2006.)

For more insightful articles from *Christianity Today* magazine, visit http://www.ctlibrary.com/ and subscribe now.

■ Open Up

Please select one of these activities to launch your discussion time.

Option 1

Discuss one of these icebreaker questions:

- Have you ever had a run-in with the law (such as a speeding ticket or getting caught toilet papering a friend's house in high school)? What punishment did you receive? Do you think it was fair or unfair? Lenient or harsh? Explain.

- When you think of "Islamic law," what images come to mind? What countries, situations, or items from the news do you think of?

- How do you feel when you hear about harsh punishments like stoning, public hanging, or decapitation in the Muslim world?

Option 2

This option requires that you have two computers with Internet access during your group time. Divide your group in two teams. Have one team do a quick five-minute Internet search on *Shari'ah* Law; the other group should also do an Internet search on (biblical) Old Testament Law. Direct each team to take notes on what they discover. The rule, though, is that they can *only* write down what they find on the Internet—they cannot supplement with information they already know.

After five minutes, gather back together and share what you discovered. Talk about these questions:

- What stands out to you most from the information you found online?

- Is there any information you expected to find but didn't?

■ The Issue

Although very few westerners have had a direct and personal experience with *Shari'ah* (Islamic law), a quick read through the books of the Law in the Old Testament will bring us face-to-face with similarly strict and extreme laws and punishments. We each must rectify our understanding of the seemingly harsh portions of Old Testament Law with the compassion and love of Jesus Christ in the New Testament.

• Have you ever talked with someone about your faith who had a problem with God's wrath as shown in the Old Testament? How did you handle it?

• Do portions of Old Testament Law cause you to struggle? If so, describe your feelings.

■ Reflect

Please read Matthew 5:17–18 and Galatians 3:19–29 on your own. Write down anything that stands out to you or questions you may have regarding these passages. How do they relate to your understanding of law and grace? What are the most important ideas here?

■ Let's Explore

The similarities between the Old Testament Law and Shari'ah can be difficult for us to accept.

• Did Paul Marshall say anything that you found surprising, interesting, or shocking? What stood out to you in his interview?

In the article, Marshall notes that:

[I]f you go through the Bible, you will also find the death penalty for idolatry. You'll find draconian punishments for adultery. You will find war in the name of God. I know of almost no Christians, even the most conservative, who believe that it's necessary to do those things in order to be a true Christian. We need to be careful not to have a double standard. There are certain things within Christianity, within Judaism, that were for a particular time. We need to allow Muslims to say the same thing.

- Is it difficult for you personally to acknowledge that some things in the Bible seem similar to Islam? Why or why not?

- Do you agree with Marshall that we appropriate a double standard between Shari'ah and Old Testament Law? Why or why not?

- How could similarities between Old Testament Law and Shari'ah be used as a bridge in conversation with Muslims? Brainstorm some creative ideas.

It may be difficult to rectify tough passages in Old Testament Law with the life of Jesus.

The Old Testament contains passages that seem harsh and may sound similar to modern-day Shari'ah. The Bible is filled with many tough passages and we'll look at two briefly. Read Leviticus 24:10–16 and Numbers 15:32–36.

- Did you know these passages were in your Bible? How do you personally feel about them?

- How would you explain passages like these in the Old Testament to a non-Christian? What might you say about the culture, the necessity of such laws, or the character of God?

Some, in their discomfort with passages like these, discount Old Testament Law, viewing it as something less than the inspired Word of God. But orthodox Christianity asserts that all of the Old Testament is part of God's Word.

- How do you harmonize passages from the Old Testament Law with what is found in the New Testament, specifically the life of Jesus?

Jesus is the fulfillment of Old Testament Law.

Read Matthew 5:17–18 in your Bible. Eugene Peterson paraphrases the passage this way in *The Message*:

Don't suppose for a minute that I have come to demolish the Scriptures— either God's Law or the Prophets. I'm not here to demolish but to complete. I am going to put it all together, pull it all together in a vast panorama.

- What does it mean that Jesus did not come to abolish the Law but to fulfill or complete it?

- If Jesus fulfills the Old Testament Law, are we still to obey laws in the Old Testament? What about the Ten Commandments? Are Christians free to do whatever we want? Explain your view.

As Christians, we live under the grace of God, not the Old Testament Law. Read Galatians 3:19–29. Here Paul explains that the Law is there to drive us to Jesus.

- How does this happen? How would you explain this from your own personal experience and interaction with Law, sin, and Jesus?

The major difference between Shari'ah and Old Testament Law is that Shari'ah has no hope of being fulfilled. But we have hope because Jesus already fulfilled the Old Testament Law by his life, death, and resurrection.

- How would you explain living under grace to a Muslim? What would be most important to share with him or her?

■ Going Forward

Take a minute to read the following quote in which Marshall explains how he thinks Christians can respond to sometimes hostile Muslim communities:

Develop strong relations with the Christian communities in those areas and find out what they need. Also, cultivate relations with Muslims in those countries and elsewhere to raise these questions. But remember that it's much more important for Muslims and Christians to talk locally. Muslims in the Middle East should talk to Christians in the Middle East.

- Why do you think it's important that Muslims and Christians talk on a local scale instead of a global scale?

- How can you create a positive and productive conversation with Muslims in your community?

Form pairs to talk about this final question:

- How has living under God's grace—rather than striving under the law—changed your life?

Take time to pray with your partner, first praising and thanking God for his grace. Then pray together for Muslims living under Shari'ah. Pray that these Muslims would come to know the grace and love of Jesus.

■ Want to Explore More?

Recommended Resources

The Book of Leviticus, New International Commentary on the Old Testament. Gordon J. Wenham (Eerdmans, 1994; ISBN 0802825222)

The Book of Numbers, New International Commentary on the Old Testament. Timothy R. Ashley (Eerdmans, 1995; ISBN 0802825230)

Five Views on Law and Gospel. Stanley N. Gundry, ed. (Zondervan, 2nd Edition, 1996, ISBN 0310212715)

The Koran (Penguin Classics, 2004; ISBN 0140449205)

Price of Honor: Muslim Women Lift the Veil of Silence on the Islamic World. Jan Goodwin (Plume, 1995, ISBN 0452274303)

Understanding Muslim Teachings and Traditions: A Guide for Christians. Phil Parshall (Baker Books, 2002; ISBN 080106418X)

Web Resources:

Answering Islam is an evangelical resource that covers a broad range of topics regarding Islam in great detail (www.answering-islam.org/).

The Global Campaign to Stop Killing and Stoning Women! is initiated by a group of lawyers, activists, journalists and academics in order to address the intensifying trend of cultural/religious legitimization of lethal violence against women (www.stop-stoning.org/).

International Campaign Against Honor Killings reports that "over five thousand women and girls are killed every year by family members in so-called 'honour killings', according to the UN. These crimes occur where cultures believe that a woman's unsanctioned sexual behaviour brings such shame on the family that any female accused or suspected must be murdered. Reasons for these murders can be as trivial as talking to a man, or as innocent as suffering rape" (www.stop-stoning.org/).

■ Notes

How can Christians find

peace amid terror?

SCRIPTURE FOCUS

Deuteronomy 7:1–11

Ephesians 6:10–18

WAR WITHOUT END

■

Practically every day since September 11, 2001, has brought news of a suicide bombing or terrorist threat somewhere in the world. As Americans attempt to understand this new situation, we receive conflicting reports about Islam—it is a religion of peace, or it has committed itself to the total destruction of the West, or it is somehow both of these things at once. What are the roots of this conflict? How can we live through a War on Terror with no rules, no escape, and no end in sight?

Using a *Christianity Today* interview with a militant Muslim cleric, "There Can Be No End to Jihad," we'll look at our place, and God's place, in this landscape of religious violence.

■ Before You Meet

Read "There Can Be No End to Jihad," interview by Anthony McRoy, from *Christianity Today* magazine. You may also want to review the appendix, "Islam 101," on p.172.

THERE CAN BE NO END TO JIHAD

Islamist Sheikh Omar Bakri Muhammad, in an exclusive interview, discusses the rationale for 9/11, the Christians he most respects, and the Jesus he defends.

Interview by Anthony McRoy

Sheikh Omar Bakri Muhammad is the leader of one of the most controversial Islamist groups in the United Kingdom, Al Muhajiroun (which means "the emigrants" in Arabic). He attracted global media scrutiny on the first anniversary of 9/11 by staging a meeting entitled "A Towering Day in History," and unveiled a poster that depicted the second airplane advancing toward the World Trade Center.

This month in Britain, Scotland Yard officials said they were investigating Sheikh Omar on suspicion of his support for "global jihad," including inciting Muslim youth to join the insurgency in Iraq. Omar, a Syrian, resides in Britain, which granted him political asylum years ago.

Omar is not a stranger to Britain's Christian community. In 1999, apologist Jay Smith of Hyde Park Christian Fellowship debated Sheikh Omar and called on him to "condemn any form of religious violence, whenever and wherever it is perpetrated in the name of God." Though differing with Smith on many issues, Omar nonetheless deeply respects him.

Christianity Today thought readers would want to better understand Omar's radical views on jihad and on his take on the Christian faith. Anthony McRoy, a London-based scholar of Islam, and a religion journalist, recently interviewed Omar Bakri Muhammad. Naturally, we don't defend Omar's views, but only present them to help Christians better understand Omar's brand of Islam, which is so prevalent in the world today.

Since the time Sheikh Omar granted this interview, he has issued a statement officially dissolving Al Muhajiroun. A later report in the Muslim Weekly, emanating from the Luton Council of Mosques (which opposes him), suggested that plans are afoot to re-brand the group as Ahl us-Sunnah wal Jamaah. Other British Muslim groups, such as the Muslim Council of Britain, frequently denounce Sheikh Omar.

Why do you believe hatred toward the United States could lead to the 9/11 attacks?

Islam is the final revelation, therefore those believing in it submit to Allah—the only One worthy of obedience in every sphere of life. To understand 9/11, we must go back to *Tawhid*—the exclusive worship of God in every sphere—religious, political, social, etc. Every human action must relate to this. 9/11 was undoubtedly an unpleasant moment for its targets or their relatives (Muslims and non-Muslim), but those committing it acted as a result of the predestined divine decree (although God does give man free will).

The "Magnificent 19" or "terrorists" are personally accountable for their actions. If these were based on God's commands, they will be rewarded; if against his commands, they will be punished.

The nineteen referred to a divine text, Surah AL-Baqara 2:190: "Fight in the way of Allah against those who fight against you . . . " Muslims believe that non-Muslims are *kaffir*—those disbelieving in Islam. This is not an insult; it is a description. The God in whom we believe did not come from the womb of a mother. The United States of America is a *kaffir* state—and *kaffir* includes those U.S. Muslims who ally with non-Muslims, e.g. in the U.S. Army, as in Iraq, and are therefore legitimate targets of jihad.

Americans should listen to Muslims who believe in 9/11 and not to those Muslims who do not! "Terrorism" can be either positive or negative—i.e., for or against God. U.S. terrorism in Iraq is anti-God. United States voters have joint liability with the government they choose, as do Russian voters in regard to the actions of their government in Chechnya—yet they voted for Putin. Complicity in the acts of one's rulers makes one a legitimate target.

America is hated because they are aggressors against Muslims in Afghanistan, Lebanon, Somalia, Iraq, Palestine, or by supporting corrupt, puppet Muslim regimes such as the Saudis, Egypt, the Gulf states, and the Shah of Iran. After World War II, America effectively declared war on Muslims and Islam—replacing the British and French Empires, controlling ex-British puppet rulers, but especially by giving military, financial, and diplomatic support to the Israelis. America uses its U.N. veto against Muslims. It establishes U.S. bases across the Muslim world—itself an act of aggression.

Do you believe that 9/11 was in any way Islamically justifiable?

Speaking objectively as a Muslim scholar, and not inciting such acts, jihad can be effected outside the battlefield—it is not restricted by time, place, building, event, people, transport food, water (both of which may be legitimately poisoned in jihad), or by clothing—there is no need to wear a uniform.

Any weapons are legitimate in jihad. Even animals may be used as "suicide bombers"! It is not restricted by target—even Muslims or children, if used by the enemy as human shields, can be killed. Only one thing can restrict jihad—a Covenant of Security [Treaty]. Non-combatant women, children, elders, clergy, insane, disabled are restricted, and non-Muslim children go to Paradise. However, if such are killed in crossfire or if used as human shields, they become collateral damage.

Again, speaking objectively as a Muslim scholar, and not inciting such acts, 9/11 was justifiable because America had no Covenant of Security with the Muslims, although Muslims in the United States are under a Covenant of Security whereby they may not act militarily against America. Only qualified scholars in *fiqh* [Islamic jurisprudence] could have planned this—because the nineteen used non-Muslim aliases to enter the country (which legally allowed them to act in jihad).

When I heard about it, I prayed to God that no Muslims in America did it because such is *haram* [forbidden in Islam]. After Al Qaeda admitted responsibility, it was obvious that qualified *ulema* [Islamic scholars] were behind it. Thus, Al-Qaeda has revived the culture of terrorism in Islam after two hundred years.

What about the hostage-taking and massacre of schoolchildren in Beslan, Russia, in September 2004?

As stated, there is no restriction on place (it could even occur in Mecca)—so schools are legitimate targets of jihad, but it is up to local mujahedeen [those who engage in jihad] to decide the best strategy.

Killing women and children never was and never will be part of the jihad in Islam, whether that be the women or children of the Muslims or non-Muslims. So if Chechen mujahedeen killed women and children in Beslan, I would condemn it. The children of non-Muslims, such as those at Beslan, who die in such circumstances go to Paradise.

Would you characterize Al Qaeda's jihad as being anti-Christian as well as being anti-American?

Al Qaeda comes from the Ahl-us Sunnah wa Jamaah sect—also known as Salafis or Al-Huruba [strangers], or "People of Tawhid" [Wahhabi branch of Islam], which explains why Zarqawi in Iraq uses the term. The jihad is not specifically anti-American.

In terms of Islamic jurisprudence, only Muslims are innocent—non-Muslims are not. By default, all non-Muslims are rebel criminals against God. Muslims who engage in interfaith [gatherings] are apostate. God discriminates among man on basis of faith. The jihad is not specifically anti-Christian—it is anti-kaffir.

Bin Laden says that his jihad is defensive. Could you explain this?

Salafis do not use these terms, but *defensive* jihad is the response to when Muslims are attacked. Offensive jihad is when Islam is brought militarily by the Islamic state in conquest, or when Muslims are arrested [for their belief].

9/11 was not an attempt to conquer America, but rather an act of retaliation. Its aim was to force America out of the Muslim world by inflicting the same pain on them as they inflict on Muslims.

Many Muslim scholars think that all Israelis, as "colonial dispossessors," but not all Americans or Russians, fit this category. What is the position of Islamic law? Is it halal (permitted by shari'ah law) to behead Western hostages in Iraq?

Women and children [i.e. boys under fifteen] or Muslims are not legitimate targets—nor are any noncombatants [clergy, disabled, insane, elderly, etc.]. Not even Israeli children or women, unless they serve in the military, which most do, or live in properties taken from dispossessed Palestinians (Muslim or Christian), which virtually all do.

However, if children are killed, the fault lies with the adult occupiers who brought them into a battlefield situation. There are two kinds of Jews in Palestine: firstly, the indigenous Palestinian Jews who always lived there with Muslims and Christians, with whom there is no problem unless they support the occupiers, and secondly, the illegitimate European colonists from Poland, Russia, etc., who are legitimate targets in jihad, because they dispossessed Muslims and covenanted [protected, indigenous] Christians.

Regarding beheading, it is *halal* to behead *Muslim* criminals! It is *halal* to kill hostages in a war zone. Regarding what can be done to secure their release, either they or their families could embrace Islam. Or, based on the principle in Islamic jurisprudence that what benefits Islam and the *Ummah* [global Muslim community] is best—such as when Salah ad-Din [Saladin] after the-recapture of Al-Quds [Jerusalem] said he would only restore the True Cross to the Crusaders if it benefited the Muslims—the relatives of hostages could offer to continually denounce the Crusades, the 1916 Sykes-Picot Agreement that divided the Middle East between the French and British, the 1917 Balfour Declaration that handed Palestine to the Zionists, U.N. Resolution 181 that established the Zionist entity, and also American government support for what the Zionist regime does to the Palestinians, as well as condemn the situations at Guantanamo Bay, Umm Qasr, Bagran, and Abu Ghraib prisons.

The *mujahedeen* then might consider that the benefits of releasing the hostages outweigh those in killing them. What happened in Spain demonstrated this: when the government announced withdrawal of troops from Iraq, the *mujahedeen* responded positively. Muslims appreciate the antiwar marches in the West. Bin Laden called on European peoples to condemn their governments.

On what basis could America have peace? Could you explain the Hudaibiyya Treaty and its implications? Is it one-off or renewable?

What the U.S. 9/11 Commission Report stated was untrue—it is not necessary for America to convert to Islam to have peace. Muslims fight America because they are aggressors; we fight apostate Muslim governments because they are aggressors against Islamic law.

Peace could come if America withdrew its forces from the Muslim world, stopped exploiting Muslim resources such as oil, have decent relationships with Muslims, and stopped supporting the Zionist aggressors and Muslim puppet governments. In other words, "Hands off Muslim lands!" Muslims did not *attack* the United States of America—the reverse is true. 9/11 was an act of *retaliation*. As Bin Laden said, peace will come when the United States withdraws from the Muslim world.

The Hudaibiyya Treaty was a ten-year truce between Muslim Medina and the pagan Meccans, and it is a basis for today. It is also renewable. It establishes a Covenant of Security. However, this is not possible with occupiers—so it could not be established with the Zionists or their supporters.

Could you explain the concepts Bin Laden employs in his statements regarding 9/11 and other events: the House of War versus the House of Faith, and the other sphere, the House of Truce or Pact? Is the latter a basis for the end of hostilities? Can jihad ever end?

Dar al-Harb, which is somewhat misleadingly translated "House of War," refers to the sphere that wars against God or Muslims. The non-Islamic domain is either at war with Muslims or under treaty. Under Dar al-Ahad—the Domain of Security—the area becomes a suspended Dar al-Harb, because treaty prevents conflict, wherein there is freedom of speech, the right of religious propagation and no military aggression.

Today there is no Dar al-Islam—the whole world is Dar al-Harb because it is the sphere of non-shari'ah. There is Dar al-Harb in terms of military aggression and occupation.

The aim of the Khilafah [Caliphate]—the ideal Islamic State, which does not presently exist—is to conquer the world, either militarily or intellectually through people converting to Islam. Under the Islamic State there is no compulsion to convert to Islam, just to have an Islamic political order. If the right of religious propagation is forbidden, the United States of America becomes Dar al-Fitnah [Domain of Persecution]. There is also Dar al-Amen, where Muslims live in non-Muslim lands under a

Covenant of Security. A Covenant of Security can be of two kinds: (1) a visa for study, asylum, etc., and (2) original Shari'ah rules whereby the norm that the lives and property of non-Muslims are lawful for Muslims to take unless they embrace Islam are removed because of a Covenant of Security.

The Mujahedeen today feel that they are like Abu Basir after the Hudaibiyya Treaty. [The treaty required Muhammad to return any man coming from Mecca. Abu Basir, a new Muslim convert, went to Medina, but was pursued by two Meccans who successfully demanded that he be handed over. On the way back he slew one of them, but Muhammad, in loyalty to his promise, refused to receive him. Then he fled to live a brigand-like life with others in his situation, killing Meccan pagans and taking their property. Eventually the Meccans asked Muhammad to receive his group into Medina]. Thus, the Mujahedeen, knowing there is no Covenant of Security, believe all lives and property to be *halal* for them. However, the norm is a treaty situation.

The United States of America ceases to be Dar al-Amen for Muslims in America if: (1) America declares Islam to be the enemy; (2) it starts arresting or killing Muslims; (3) it bans Islamic preaching. Muslims are not allowed to fight America from within its borders when they normally live there—they must leave and then fight.

There can be no end to jihad—a *hadith* [narration of Muhammad] states this, but treaties can be a form of jihad. An example is the treaty relationship established between Medina and the Christian state of Najran, or the Jewish entity of Khaybar, where both were self-governing, but within Dar al-Islam.

You have talked about the Islamic flag flying over Downing Street, and I have seen a hadith on your Web site saying that the end would not come until the White House is captured. How do you envisage these goals being achieved?

"The final hour will not come until the Muslims conquer the White House" is a hadith related by Tabarani, a great Muslim scholar. How?

The Khilafah is necessary for offensive jihad, though it could occur if Muslims warred to liberate captive Muslims. Realistically, it will probably occur through intellectual da'wah [Islamic missionary activity].

How would a Caliphate operate?

Under the *Khilafah*, authority is centralized, but not administration. The Caliph appoints ministers, judges, governors, army commanders, etc. Constitutionally, although all analogies are imperfect, the *Khilafah* is closer to the U.S. presidential system than to the U.K. parliamentary system with a Prime Minister, although the major difference is that the Caliph operates under a divine mandate.

There could be no non-Muslim judges. Effectively, the Qur'an and Sunnah [practice and narrations of Muhammad related in Hadith] are the Constitution, Shari'ah is the law. The Caliph is chosen by Muslims, whether by popular election, or selection by Majlis as-Shura [Consultative Assembly]. Non-Muslims can enter the Majlis to represent their own community.

What would be the rights of Christians in a restored Caliphate?

As citizens, in terms of welfare and security, education, etc., they will be equal. They will be exempt from national service, although they can volunteer. They will pay the *Jizya* poll-tax for security and signifying that they submit to Islamic law, except if they join the army. This need not be levied with humiliation. Nor is it levied on women, children, clergy, elderly, etc., only on mature, working males.

No private schools will be allowed, and there will be an Islamically influenced national curriculum. No new churches will be permitted, but existing ones will be allowed. Private consumption of alcohol will be permitted, but not its public sale. All state officials must be Muslims, save for the Caliph's assistants to advise him about relations with non-Muslim citizens. Muslims could not convert to Christianity on pain of execution. Evangelistic campaigns would be forbidden, but people would be free to present Christianity on TV, in debates, etc.

You have debated American evangelicals like Jay Smith. Do you only believe in debating or do you see a place for dialogue?

Debate and dialogue is the same. A treaty is dialogue. No inter-faith; religions are not the same. Debate is fine.

Talking of Jay, what do you think of him and other evangelicals that you have met?

I feel very comfortable with Jay—with him, what you see is what you get. He is no hypocrite, and neither are Salafis. His words and actions match his heart. He does not pretend by saying soft words about Islam. The Qur'an calls for debate.

Specifically, what do you think of U.S. evangelicals?

Most U.S. evangelicals refuse to debate Muslims, unlike the courage of Jay who boldly cries "Jesus is Lord!" I am always willing to meet him. However, I have no direct experience of most U.S. evangelicals, and I will not judge on the basis of what I see on TV. I am always skeptical of television.

You issued a fatwa some years ago sentencing the U.S. author of the "blasphemous" play Corpus Christi to death. What do you think of Christ?

In Islam, Jesus is called Al-Masih 'Isa [the Messiah Jesus]. He is a Messenger of Allah, miraculously born of the Virgin Mary. He spoke in the cradle, defended the message of previous prophets—Noah, Abraham, Moses, etc., preached the oneness of God, predicted the coming of a prophet called Ahmed [i.e., Muhammad], he denied the Trinity and being Son of God.

He will return before the Day of Judgment, and will be a Sign of the Hour. He will judge between Muslims and Christians, abolish jihad because his presence will be the point of conflict with the Dajjal [Antichrist], who will fight, allied with Jews and false Christians, against the Mahdi [Rightly-Guided one expected in Islamic eschatology] and Jesus.

The fatwa against the author of *Corpus Christi* was because it was an attack on Jesus, which is the same as an attack on Muhammad and God. Muslims have a duty to defend Jesus.

Anthony McRoy is an Islamic studies experts, religion journalist, and a lecturer at the Evangelical Theological College of Wales.

("There Can Be No End to Jihad" was originally published online at www. christianitytoday.com in February 2005.)

For more insightful articles from *Christianity Today* magazine, visit http://www. ctlibrary.com/ and subscribe now.

■ Open Up

Select one of these activities to launch your discussion time.

Option 1

Discuss one of these icebreaker questions:

• How do you feel when you hear news about acts of terrorism? What thoughts or emotions do you experience?

• Where did you first encounter the word jihad? What does it mean to you?

• How does this article make you feel?

Option 2

Imagine yourself in Anthony McRoy's place, with an opportunity to interview a militant Muslim leader.

- What would you wear to the interview? How and where would you conduct it? How might you feel in the moments leading up to the first question?

- What questions would you ask, in addition to those McRoy asked? Did he ask any questions you would not have asked?

- What would you hope to gain from the interview? What would you hope to give, to your interviewee as well as to your audience?

■ The Issue

This interview contains many sobering, and possibly frightening, thoughts for American Christians. Sheikh Omar Bakri Muhammad envisions Muslims conquering the White House and instituting a regime under which all Americans—indeed, all people—submit to Islamic law and send their children to Islamically influenced schools. Any man, woman, or child who stands in the way of this vision is a fair target for terrorism. Many Muslims denounce this way of thinking, but many others, including the 9/11 hijackers, apparently agree with it.

- On a scale of 0 (least) to 100 (most), how worried are you about Sheikh Muhammad's vision becoming reality?

- On the same scale, how much does the concept of a total war between the West and Islam impinge on your life right now? How much does this concept color your understandings of Islam, global politics, and world missions?

■ Reflect

Take a few moments to read Deuteronomy 7:1–11 and Ephesians 6:10–18. First, note your initial impression of each passage and write down any questions the passage might raise. Then, analyze the battle each passage describes: who is fighting, when, where, how (with what armaments), and why.

■ Let's Explore

God's people have always faced fearsome enemies.

Militant Islam might be the most terrifying threat any of us has faced in our lifetimes. Communists spoke of world domination but never treated every street corner and shopping mall on the planet as a war zone. Nazis pursued a deadly agenda, with horrific results, but their menace rose and fell in little over a decade; Islam has challenged Christians and Jews for fourteen hundred years. The size and scope of the Islamic threat can arouse panic, the feeling that we must do something right now to get everything back to "normal." But conflict is "normal" for human history, and God's people live on the front lines.

- Where have so many American Christians gotten the idea that peace and prosperity are "normal"? What dangers does this idea pose?

One of the more puzzling verses in the New Testament is Matthew 10:34, in which Jesus, the Prince of Peace, announces, "Do not suppose that I have come to bring peace to the earth. I did not come to bring peace, but a sword" (NIV). In context, the statement refers to the battle between good and evil that has raged since Satan's fall and will continue to the end of time. That battle is also the context for the quite different conflicts described in Deuteronomy 7:1–11 and Ephesians 6:10–18. Revisit those passages in light of Jesus's statement.

• Why would peace be impossible in either of the situations described in these passages?

• Look back at the interview. Under what conditions does Sheikh Muhammad consider peace with the West possible? Under what conditions (if any) would you, as a Christian, consider peace with Islam possible?

All battles are the Lord's.

Just before David felled Goliath, he predicted his victory and proclaimed to the Philistines, "All those gathered here will know that it is not by sword or by spear that the Lord saves; for the battle is the Lord's, and he will give all of you into our hands" (1 Samuel 17:47 NIV). With the largest economy, most formidable nuclear arsenal, and best-equipped armed forces in the world, it can be difficult for Americans to think of themselves as David, who fought a giant foe with little more than bare hands. Yet Christians must remember that we have no strength apart from God.

- The prime mover in both of our passages is the Lord (see Deuteronomy 7:1 and Ephesians 6:10). Look back through the passages and highlight what God does (especially in Deuteronomy) and what he provides (especially in Ephesians). Share with each other what you observe.

- God expresses his sovereignty very differently in the physical conflicts of Deuteronomy 7 and the spiritual conflicts of Ephesians 6. How can we understand him to be equally sovereign in both cases?

- Is it natural for you to think of God as a warrior? How is this image comforting or distressing to you?

Our primary responsibility in wartime is to live out ordinary faith.

In the article, Sheikh Muhammad says a great deal about what Muslims can, should, must, and must not do in the prosecution of jihad. It would be difficult to find a contemporary Christian leader giving such detailed and absolute directions about wartime conduct. Christians do not believe that God's instructions to the Israelites in passages like Deuteronomy 7:1–5 still apply to us today, and passages like Ephesians 6:10–18 admit many different interpretations. Nonetheless, the latter verses of these passages offer clear guidance for everyday life even today: remember God's love, follow his commands, and pray.

- How do God's words, spoken through Moses, in Deuteronomy 7:6–11 apply to you? Do you find it difficult to read yourself into this story, even with the first five verses of the chapter bracketed out? Why or why not?

- After his elaborate metaphor of the armor of God, Paul gives concrete directions in Ephesians 6:18. Why do you think Paul wanted his "last word" on this subject to be an exhortation to prayer?

■ Going Forward

Break into pairs and discuss these next questions.

- What would you need to do, mentally and in practice, to "put on the full armor of God" every day?

- How is this preparation similar to and different from a Muslim's pursuit of jihad?

Gather back together as a group; together make a list of prayers appropriate to the context of religious war. Directly or indirectly quote Scripture wherever possible, such as psalms and prophets as well as the New Testament. Pray through the list together.

■ Want to Explore More?

Recommended Resources

Between Pacifism and Jihad: Just War and Christian Tradition, J. Daryl Charles (InterVarsity Press, 2005; ISBN 0830827722)

Islam and Terrorism: What the Quran Really Teaches, Mark A. Gabriel (Frontline, 2002; ISBN 0884198847)

Christianity and Islam, DVD (Vision Video, 2004; ISBN 1563647982)

Understanding Muslim Teaching and Traditions: A Guide for Christians, Phil Parshall (Baker, 2002; ISBN 080106418X)

Perspectives on War in the Bible, John Wood (Mercer Press, 1998; ISBN 0865545642)

■ Notes

How are we to relate to

Muslims and other people

groups during a time of

such misunderstanding and

disconnection?

SCRIPTURE FOCUS	
Leviticus 19:33–35	
Deuteronomy 10:17–19	
Acts 1:6–9	

THE GLOBAL GOSPEL: BATTLING PREJUDICE AND ISOLATIONISM

■

What all of us consider a tragedy, a great disaster, and a terrible evil can also be seen as a wake-up call, says Miriam Adeney in response to the September 11 attacks on the World Trade Center. Worldwide e-mail as well as the goods we buy may link us to people all around the world, but many of us continue to live "cocooned in our own little circle of friends, walled off from people who are different," Adeney says.

And in many cases, this sense of self-protection and disconnection from other cultural groups also includes a latent but virulent prejudice against Muslims. Examples of anti-Muslim bias can be seen throughout pop culture, from harsh language on radio talk shows to repeated portrayals of Muslims as terrorists in movies and television. This hidden prejudice can also creep into *our* lives, expressed in light-hearted comments about someone with a full-beard as "looking like" a terrorist or a sense of unease (or outright fear) when someone in Middle-Eastern dress boards our plane.

Fear, ignorance, and prejudice toward Muslims is hurtful to the gospel message. Our disconnection from Muslims and other cultural groups around the world is not only detrimental to the future of our nation but also is not faithful to the biblical vision for humanity.

■ Before You Meet

Please read the article "A Wake-Up Call to Become Global Christians" by Miriam Adeney from *Christianity Today* before your discussion.

A WAKE-UP CALL TO BECOME GLOBAL CHRISTIANS

The deadly attacks on America will provoke many responses, but Christians are commanded to love our neighbors.

By Miriam Adeney

How do we respond to the devastation of September 11, deadly attacks on the World Trade Center and the Pentagon? Many responses come to mind. Prayer. Care for the injured and bereft. Increased security, increased vigilance. Just punishment for the masterminds behind the carnage, if we can find them. Sharper on-the-ground intelligence-gathering. Stronger international cooperation against terrorism. Congregational immersion in Scripture stories of God's people who lived through radical loss and destabilization, from Joseph to Daniel to John, Peter, and Paul.

Hit in the Solar Plexus

This disaster is a wake-up call. Since the so-called end of the Cold War, many of us have not given much thought to the rest of the world except as occasional business, tourist, or short-term mission connections. Those days are over. We've been hit in the solar plexus with the truth that that we are globally connected and cannot cut loose.

Businessmen already know that. In Thomas Friedman's bestseller on globalization, *The Lexus and the Olive Tree,* he describes a label on a computer part that reads, "This part was made in Malaysia, Singapore, the Philippines, China, Mexico, Germany, the United States, Thailand, Canada, and Japan. It was made in so many different places that we cannot specify a country of origin." Through the Internet many Americans have also tapped into a common global shopping system and global library. We are globally integrated as never before.

Yet many of us continue to live cocooned in our own little circle of friends, walled off from people who are different. To think about the rest of the world overwhelms us. Masses of data pour out of the media, jumbled in sound bites that juxtapose great human tragedies with beer ads. We know Americans overseas have made mistakes. We know missionaries have. How can ordinary citizens like you and me know enough to make intelligent comments on global issues?

"Whenever I think about those people over there, I worry," says my friend Susan. "And I know God doesn't want me to be worried. So I've decided he doesn't want me to think about them." Another friend named Janet says that's why she doesn't read the newspaper anymore. The news disturbs her, and surely that isn't the will of God.

Our Ignorance Has Come Home to Haunt Us

In this we reflect our society's disconnect from the rest of the world. Consider this. Well before the World Trade Center bombing in 1993, where six people were killed and more than one thousand injured, the FBI was in possession of some of the plans. The Agency held videotapes, manuals, and notebooks on bomb making that had been seized from one of the plotters. They also had taped phone conversations in which one terrorist told another how to build the bomb.

"There was one problem: They were in Arabic. And nobody who understood Arabic listened to them until after the explosion at the Trade Center," according to *New York Times* reporter Diana Schemo.

Last year all the colleges and universities in the United States graduated only nine students who majored in Arabic. There is a joke making the rounds:

What do you call a person who speaks three languages?

Trilingual.

What do you call a person who speaks two languages?

Bilingual.

What do you call a person who speaks one language?

American.

Now our ignorance has come home to haunt us.

Pray Through the Newspaper

Of all people, Christians are to love our neighbors. When our neighborhood expands to include the globe, then we're called to love globally. How? Some of the most important steps may be some of the simplest.

Pray through the newspaper, especially the world news section. Befriend the foreigners who live in your city. Develop strong relationships with your church or denominational missionaries.

Ask members who are businessmen to talk about their global involvements. Go to the local college and find out whether there's a group of local "friends of international students." Do the same with the Chamber of Commerce and foreign businessmen.

Ask your high school and college youth what they're studying about global issues. Teach a church class on the biblical basis of mission, tracing global issues from Genesis to Revelation.

Those who want more can find hundreds of mission-related sites on the Internet. Some useful gateways include www.brigada.org and www.lausanne.org.

If you want to know more about specific nations or ethnic groups, you might try some of the general search engines (AltaVista, Yahoo!, Northern Light, or Hotbot), or the Joshua Project List of People Group Profiles (www.joshuaproject.net/index.php).

Mission magazines with online resources include *Evangelical Missions Quarterly,* (bgc.gospelcom.net/emis/emqpg.htm) and the International Bulletin of Missionary Research (www.gospel.com).

Apples, Salmon, Hungry Bellies, and Empty Arms

Yet we can do all this with a patronizing smile, at arms' length—without ever leaving the security of our own turf. Loving our neighbors means something more. It means being vulnerable. It means entering into their pain. When God in Jesus came to live among us, he shared our troubles and felt our hurts. Do we feel the pain of those in other countries?

Globalization has hurt a lot of people. That includes Americans. Last weekend my husband and I drove through the apple orchards of Washington. In spite of their rows of green trees heavy with fruit beside the Columbia River, 20 percent of those farmers are failing.

Some blame cheaper apples from Mexico and China.

Apple season coincides with salmon season, and we have not had such a glorious run of fish since the 1960s. Yet the commercial fishermen are giving the fish away, or mailing them to state legislators. They can't make a profit. The price is too low. Some blame competition from farm-raised salmon from Chile.

The transitions and readjustments of globalization can hurt Americans. But people in other countries suspect that transnational corporations—most based in America—are reaping the lion's share of the benefits. This breeds a love/hate feeling toward America.

Yong-Hun Jo of Korea, in the article, "Globalization as a Challenge to the Churches in Asia Today," published in the October 2000 issue of the *Asian Journal of Theology,* says poverty levels in Asian countries have worsened as globalization has bloomed. Although the article's tone is moderate and recognizes the benefits of a vigorous economy, it also speaks of bankruptcies, destruction of jobs, massive unemployment, a sharp rise in prices and decline in wages, capital flight into tax-free zones, the reduction of public services, environmental degradation, and a growing distance between the rich and the poor. At present 34 percent of the children under age five in Southeast Asia are under weight, and 50 percent of the children in South Asia. Half the people in the world live on two dollars a day or less. Meanwhile, there is a "race to the bottom," as companies vie to see who can pay workers least, offering the fewest benefits. If one country does insist on safeguards for its workers, multinational capital departs for a neighboring state in a matter of hours.

Melba Maggay in *Patmos: Journal of the Institute for the Study of Asian Church and Culture* speaks of the cost to families when labor must follow jobs in a borderless world. Filipinos, Maggay's compatriots, are thick on the ground as laborers, managers, and nannies in the Middle East, and as maids in Hong Kong and Singapore. Back home they may leave spouses and children, not to mention parents with whom traditionally they would have spent much time. Globalization obliterates that family closeness.

Complacent on Our Couches

Do we feel that pain? The prophet Amos blasted God's people because they did not grieve for hurting people.

"Woe to you who are complacent in Zion and to you who feel secure on Mount Samaria, you notable men of the foremost nation. . . You lie on beds inlaid with ivory and lounge on your couches, You dine on choice lambs . . .You improvise on musical instruments . . . but you do not grieve over the ruin of Joseph" (Amos 6:1–6 NIV).

In one sense this text refers to a special case. In a broader sense, it may serve as a wake-up call for us. Do we grieve for those who hurt outside our borders? "Suppose a brother or sister is without clothes and daily food," writes the author of the Epistle of James. "If one of you says to him, 'Go, I wish you well; keep warm and well fed,' but does nothing about his physical needs, what good is it? In the same way, faith by itself, if it is not accompanied by action, is dead" (2:15–17 NIV).

Even if we limit the application of this text to Christians, in all 238 countries of the world today there are Christians, according to the *World Christian Encyclopedia.* And surely we ought to love non-Christians concretely too?

There are many macrostructural and microstructural ways to reach out to these needs, but they are beyond the scope of this essay. Evangelism remains primary. Economic programs may teach methods, but evangelism will unleash the meaning and the motivation to use those methods conscientiously.

The Earth Is Whose?

How shall we respond to the devastation of September 11? Our government and military will need to respond at several levels. We could discuss justice and retribution and security and Israel and Palestine. If we have been cozy and complacent Christians, this tragedy also is a personal wake-up call. There's a big, real world out there. It is not negligible. India's population alone is larger—by two hundred million—than the entire Western Hemisphere. China's population is larger than the entire Western world—all of Europe and North America combined. We cannot indefinitely ignore the pains of other peoples without danger to ourselves—from huge hungry populations, from environmental degradation, from terrorism. For reasons of security alone we must pay attention to the world. Current levels of global inequality are unsustainable.

More important, the earth is the Lord's. All of Scripture rings with this. God's concern for global issues didn't begin when Jesus said, "Go into all the world" or "You shall be my witnesses." Thousands of years earlier, Abraham heard God call his name, saying, "I will bless you, and in you all the families of the earth will be blessed" (Gen. 12:2,3 NKJV). David's psalms sing out: "May God be gracious to us and bless us . . . that your way may be known upon earth, your saving power among all nations" (Ps. 67:1–2 NRSV).

Isaiah saw the people of God as a light to the nations (42:6). Habakkuk saw the "earth full of the knowledge of the Lord as the waters cover the sea" (2:14 NIV). Micah saw that "His greatness will reach to the ends of the earth. And He will be their peace" (5:4–5 NIV). Jonah, Daniel, Esther, Nehemiah, and even Naaman's little slave girl saw God's care for the nations. All of Scripture resonates with God's absorbing interest in the whole earth. We cannot be healthy American Christians today and ignore the world. A global concern is not optional. It comes from the heart of God.

How shall we respond to the devastation of September 11? In his brief commentary on Revelation titled *For the Healing of the Nations,*

Justo Gonzalez paints two alternative pictures. Glimpsing them may help us find a place to stand. First:

There is a vision according to which all peoples and nations and tribes and languages must bow before the beast and worship it. This is the vision of Nebuchadnezzar: "You are commanded, O peoples, nations, and languages, that . . . you are to fall down and worship the golden statue that King Nebuchadnezzar has set up" (Dan. 3:4–5 NIV). There is a vision that takes for granted that there will always be a great harlot who sits upon many waters; and these waters are the many nations and tribes and languages and peoples who must bring their wealth to her. In a way, this is the vision of Belshazzar in the book of Daniel, who does not learn from his father's humiliation, but is content with inheriting his power over peoples and nations. If we live by that vision, we shall be content with a world order in which many nations and tribes and peoples and cultures have no other purpose in life but to enrich those who sit upon many waters. According to that vision, the nations and peoples and tribes can and should remain subjected, for that is their place in the scheme of things. According to that vision, our task is to make sure that we, and others like us, are the ones who sit upon many waters, while the rest of the world enriches us.

But that is not the vision of John of Patmos. According to his vision, out of these many nations and tribes and peoples and languages, God will build a kingdom in which all have royal and priestly honor. According to that vision, a great multitude, from all different nations and cultures, will jointly sing, "Holy, Holy, Holy, Lord God Almighty." According to that vision, our music and our worship must be multicultural, not simply because our society is multicultural, but because the future from which God is calling us is multicultural. We must be multicultural, not just so that those from other cultures may feel at home among us, but also so that we may feel at home in God's future . . . because like John of Patmos, our eyes have seen the glory of the coming of the Lord; because we know and we believe that on that great waking-up morning when the stars begin to fall, when we gather at the river where angel feet have trod, we shall all, from all nations and tribes and peoples and languages, we shall all sing without ceasing: "Holy, holy, holy! All the saints adore thee, casting down our golden crowns before the glassy sea; cherubim and seraphim; Japanese and Swahili; American and European; Cherokee and Ukrainian; falling down before thee, who wert, and art, and evermore shall be! Amen!" (Orbis, 1999, pp.111–112).

Miriam Adeney is editor at large for *Christianity Today* and is Associate Professor of World Christian Studies at Seattle Pacific University.

("A Wake-Up Call to Become Global Christians" was first published in *Christianity Today*, October 22, 2001, pp. 14–15.)

For more insightful articles from *Christianity Today* magazine, visit http://www.ctlibrary.com/ and subscribe now.

■ Open Up

Select one of these activities to launch your discussion time.

Option 1

Discuss one of these icebreaker questions:

- Have you ever been in a situation when you felt someone unfairly stereotyped you? Describe that experience.

- Prejudice and racism are highly-charged words. What thoughts or feelings do they stir up in you? What images or experiences immediately come to mind when you hear the words prejudice or racism?

- Have you ever had a conversation with someone who you consider to be prejudiced? Describe that person's prejudice. Why does he or she feel that way? Is his or her perspective justifiable? Why or why not?

Option 2

Have a group member read these statements aloud while you each silently think of your own response to them:

1. Should airport security screeners more closely scrutinize those whose dress or appearance looks Middle-Eastern or Muslim?

2. Should the police or other law enforcement agencies infiltrate Muslim religious groups and civic organizations to spy on their meetings and use of funds?

3. Should the government use racial profiling against Muslims and others from the Middle East?

4. Should American Muslims have to register and carry special ID cards so the government can keep a close watch on them?

Read the following together:

A USA TODAY/Gallup Poll (in 2006) found that 39 percent of Americans feel they have some degree of prejudice or bias against Muslims. One in five Americans reported they would not want to have Muslim neighbors. Nearly two in five Americans said they want Muslims to carry special ID cards. And according to a Cornell University report (in 2004), one in four Americans think the government should closely monitor mosques while 29 percent of Americans think that undercover agents should infiltrate Muslim groups to keep tabs on their activities. Almost half of all respondents to the poll asserted that civil liberties for Muslim Americans should be curtailed for the sake of preventing terrorism.

- What's your response to these findings? How do they compare or contrast with your own views?

Re-read the numbered statements above aloud as a group, replacing the word *Muslim* with *Christian*.

- What would it be like to live in a society in which many people held these views about you?

■ The Issue

Adeney begins her article with the question, "How do we respond to the devastation of September 11, deadly attacks on the World Trade Center and the Pentagon?" Several years after her article's publication, we can look back and see a variety of responses to what happened that day. Adeney answers her own question, saying:

Many responses come to mind. Prayer. Care for the injured and bereft. Increased security, increased vigilance. Just punishment for the masterminds behind the carnage, if we can find them. Sharper on-the-ground intelligence-gathering. Stronger international cooperation against terrorism. Congregational immersion in Scripture stories of God's people who lived through radical loss and destabilization, from Joseph to Daniel to John, Peter, and Paul.

Some have responded to the terrorist attacks and the war on terror with an effort to connect cross-culturally and tear down divisions between the West and the Middle East. Many others, however, have responded—directly or inadvertently—with increased isolationism and prejudice.

- Which response have you observed most commonly in your community or your church? A positive response geared toward outreach? Or a negative response focusing inward and resulting in prejudice or isolationism? Explain.

■ Reflect

Read Leviticus 19:33–35; Deuteronomy 10:17–19; and Acts 1:6–9 on your own. Take notes about the key ideas and how they relate to our culture today. What questions do they bring up? What challenges do they bring to the modern reader?

■ Let's Explore

Prejudice against Muslims or others who are different from us has no place among God's people.

The word *prejudice* comes from the Latin *praejudicium* which means "prior judgment." In the wake of 9/11 and during the ongoing "war on terror," many American Muslims have experienced varying degrees of anti-Muslim prejudice.

• Put yourself in an American Muslim's shoes for a moment and imagine what it might be like to be the recipient of anti-Muslim bias. What "prior judgments" do you imagine people would make about you? What examples of stereotyping in pop culture might be hurtful to you? In what types of situations do you imagine you might be treated with prejudice?

• What do you see as the main cause of this type of prejudice? Is it fear? Anger? Ignorance? Explain.

The Council on American-Islamic Relations (CAIR) addresses this issue, calling it *Islamophobia.* CAIR defines *Islamophobia* this way on their Web site (www.cair.com):

Islamophobia refers to unfounded fear of and hostility towards Islam. Such fear and hostility leads to discriminations against Muslims, exclusion of Muslims from mainstream political or social process, stereotyping, the presumption of guilt by association, and finally hate crimes. In twenty-first century America, all of these evils are present and in some quarters tolerated. While America has made major progress in racial harmony, there is still a long road ahead of us to reach our destination when all people are judged on the content of their character and neither on the color of their skin or their faith.

• What's your response to CAIR's definition? Do you agree with their critique of American culture? Why or why not?

Revisit Leviticus 19:33–35 and Deuteronomy 10:17–19.

• In the Old Testament context, why do you think it was so important to God that the Israelites treat aliens and foreigners with love and dignity?

• In today's context, Muslims—even those who are American citizens—are often treated as outsiders. What would it look like for Christians to live out the principles of Leviticus 19:33–35 and Deuteronomy 10:17–19 in our society? Share examples and ideas.

We are called to be globally-minded Christians, lovingly sharing out the Good News to all cultural groups and nationalities.

John 3:16 reveals the heart of Jesus' mission: "God loved the [whole] world so much that he gave his one and only Son so that whoever believes in him may not be lost, but have eternal life." Motivated by a deep and enduring love, Jesus reached out to people despite their gender, race, or national identity.

- Jesus often got into trouble for crossing over the cultural boundaries and divisions between Gentiles and Jews, rich and poor, men and women, sinners and righteous, and so on. What are some biblical examples of this that come to mind for you?

After his resurrection, Christ commanded his disciples to go into the world, making disciples of all nations (see Matthew 28:18–20). By sending his disciples into the world, Christ gathers a new people, a new nation, the kingdom of God, whereby God's first and last intentions for humanity will be achieved. Those intentions are being achieved today via the spread of the Christian faith, in which race, gender, and nationality count for nothing (see Galatians 3:26–29). What counts is the expansive, inclusive, all-embracing reach of Christ.

Read Acts 1:6–9. The book of Acts portrays the church as a kind of wildfire that spreads the good news of Christ throughout the world. The gospel is not to be restricted to the first people who hear the good news of Christ. It is not to be kept safe in Israel or Rome or any one nation. It must go to "Judea, Samaria, and the ends of the earth."

From the beginning, the church has been thrust into the world. From the beginning, the gospel is meant to leap over all boundaries, to intrude into every culture. The church in every age must learn this lesson. We are not permitted to hunker down with folks just like us. Jesus is busy reaching out to everyone. If we would be like Jesus, we must reach out as well.

- On a scale of 1 to 10 (1 being awful and 10 being fantastic), how well do you think the church is doing when it comes to being Christ's witness to the Muslim world? Explain. (Consider this question both in terms of international missions as well as how it might apply to the Muslims living in your local community.)

- What are some ways in which your church is going into the world and crossing cultural boundaries as witnesses of Jesus's message? What are some ideas for other ways your church might be more globally minded, specifically in outreach to Muslims?

■ Going Forward

Break into pairs to discuss these final questions:

Martin Luther King Jr. famously said this of the civil rights struggle in America: "We will remember not the words of our enemies, but the silence of our friends."

- Is the church guilty of being "silent" when it comes to mistreatment of Muslims or prejudice against those of Middle-Eastern descent? What actions do you think Christians ought to take in order to better reflect God's justice and love?

In an editorial about Christian outreach to Muslims, the editors of *Christianity Today* welcomed the pioneering work of missionaries in the Middle East. But they also pointed out that:

[T]here is more for American Christians to do. Acknowledging our need for contrition and repentance is a good place to start. A 1978 Lausanne report on Muslim evangelism noted the tragic lack of progress in Muslim outreach: "We Christians have loved so little and have put forth such little effort to regard Muslims as people like ourselves." More recently, Frontiers, AIMS (Accelerating International Mission Strategies), and other Muslim-focused missions issued a declaration of "Christian Attitudes Toward Muslims," which says in part, "We are guilty of believing and perpetuating misconceptions, prejudice, and, in some cases, hostility and outright hatred toward Muslim peoples." But this statement also declares, "Reconciliation is the goal of our repentance" and sets out an agenda of prayer, compassion, and interaction with Muslims.

- In what areas do you feel challenged or convicted when it comes to your own mind-set, attitude, actions (or lack of actions) toward Muslims? Do you feel you feel you have "loved so little"? Explain.

- Adeney highlights several practical and important ways we can better live as global Christians. What's one life application challenge that stood out to you from her article? How will you implement it in your life in the coming week?

Gather back together as a group for a time of prayer; follow Miriam Adeney's suggestion to "pray through the newspaper." Pass out copies of several newspapers and make a list of world crises or needs of people in other countries. Pay particular attention to situations affecting Muslims.

Close with prayers asking God to intercede in each one of these needs. Thank God for his work in the world, and ask him for guidance on further ways in which we can individually and corporately reach out to a world full of people who need to hear the good news of Christ.

■ Want to Explore More?

Recommended Resources

Learn about the a Muslim perspective of prejudice and civil rights issues at www. cair.com.

Who Speaks For Islam?: What a Billion Muslims Really Think, John L. Esposito and Dalia Mogahed (Gallup Press, 2008; ISBN: 1595620176)

Brides to Islam: A Christian Perspective on Folk Islam, Phil Parshall (Authentic Press, 2007; ISBN 1932805826)

■ Notes

How can we build a bridge

to Muslims in order to bring

them back across to Jesus?

SCRIPTURE FOCUS

Luke 10:25–37

BUILDING A BRIDGE

■

There is a gaping chasm that exists between
Christians and Muslims; it often appears
threatening, dark, and innavigable. But as we'll
explore in this study, it is possible to bridge the divide
and introduce Muslims to Jesus. In most cases, the bridge
building takes place over several years and is packed with
varied experiences for the Muslim involved. Yet other rare
times God just uses a few conversations or a copy of the
New Testament to prepare a Muslim to accept Jesus as his
or her Savior. Are you ready for the long haul of sharing
the love of Jesus with a Muslim you know over many years?
This study will examine the article "Engaging Our Muslim
Neighbors" by Wendy Murray Zoba; it's a great resource
to help us prepare to reach out to Muslims and start
building that bridge, no matter how long it may take.

1
2
3
4
5
6
7
8

■ Before You Meet

Please read the article "Engaging Our Muslim Neighbors" by Wendy Murray Zoba from *Christianity Today* before your discussion. You may also want to review the appendix, "Islam 101," on p.172.

ENGAGING OUR MUSLIM NEIGHBORS

The church faces a challenge not just to understand Muslims, but to befriend them.

By Wendy Murray Zoba

The South Asian Friendship Center is a bookstore in the heart of a Muslim business district in Chicago. (More than 400,000 Muslims live in Chicago.) The shelves are lined with books in Urdu (the language of Pakistan), Arabic, and English with author names like J. I. Packer and John Stott. The center makes no apologies for its overt Christian beliefs.

SAFC, a multidenominational effort of many area churches, opened in September 1997 and carries out a fourfold vision. First, SAFC's bookstore is a legitimate business. A "mini-Borders" for Asians, it is a haven where people can read and relax on a couch or other chairs, nibbling on free cookies and sipping *chai* (Indian tea). SAFC sells Christian literature, books, videos, and cassettes at reasonable prices—and often gives these items away.

Second, SAFC strives to serve the community by offering tutoring in English as a second language; after-school homework help; classes in Hindu and Urdu; help with immigration issues; legal counsel; home visitation; and medical help.

The third aspect of SAFC's vision is what staff members call passive evangelism: "People come to us and we pray with people unashamedly in the name of Jesus," says Roy Oksnevad, director of training and development. He describes how one Muslim man desperately needed a job. SAFC workers asked if they could pray for him in Jesus's name. "I really like this place," the man said before he left. "You are our friends."

Fourth, SAFC trains students, missionaries, and churches that want to develop similar ministries. The SAFC sponsors weekend "vision trips" for people to learn about the center and visit a mosque or Hindu temple to expose them to the need. The SAFC also will send staff members to speak in churches.

"In this country, I'm not worried about what Muslims are doing," says SAFC director Sam Naaman. "I know what they are doing. They are active—far more active than we Christians are." That's why we started the center. We have to be out on the street. These people who are passing by and see the Scripture portions from the door, they cannot say when the Lord comes, 'I didn't know about Christianity.' "

Naaman is worried, however, about what Muslims are doing in his home country, Pakistan. When his father was actively distributing Christian literature and evangelizing, people threatened to harm his family or to kill him if he did not stop. "My father was [once] a fundamentalist Muslim who fought for Islam. It was not easy for him to get scared by these threats," Naaman says. "But I think he underestimated the threat." Muslims killed his brother Obed, twenty-six, in 1990. "It was very unexpected. He was a devout born-again Christian who wanted to serve the Lord in our country." The death of his brother plays a major role in Naaman's motivation to minister to Muslims today. "When the best thing you have is taken from you—you ask yourself, 'What else is there to give up for the Lord? A brother is like your arms. His sacrifice will never be in vain. Once you have given up everything for the Lord, I don't think anything can stop you.'"

The SAFC incarnates key principles that apply to any Western Christian attempting to befriend Muslims.

These include:

- Take the initiative. "If you want to encounter Islam, you have to go where they are. That's where we are going to face Islam—not in our churches, but on the street," Naaman says. "My dream is to have a center like this in every city in the United States." (SAFC has opened another center in New York and is working on one for Toronto.)

- Be bold, yet loving, about our faith in Jesus. "Let's not be too humble. Let's not apologize for believing in Christ," Naaman says. "Let's stand very strongly on our faith and practice what we preach. With all due respect, the Western church is very naïve. You talk about contextualizing and befriending Muslims—and I have no problem with that—but I also know that Islam is a religion of power. You have to become strong—confront them in love—but be very strict that this is our faith and that Jesus is the only way. If that doesn't happen, we just make fun of ourselves."

- Encourage Christian women to get involved. "Women will play a major role" in affecting Islamic cultures, Naaman says. "As a woman, you can go and enter the inner section of the house. You can have a cup of tea or you can cook with her. You can make conversation with her and she will open up to you." There is "a wall of genders in Islam," he says, which means that sometimes a Muslim woman can relate more closely to a Christian woman than to her husband. "Once the husband knows that you really care for his wife and that, as a Christian, you don't like the sin in American society then—boom—the bond is there. Once the bond is there, once he knows that you really take time, you will see—they will break down in tears and cry. You will get more dishes from her side than you can keep up with." The SAFC also serves as a new model for missions: using the gifts and talents of trained and seasoned missionaries here in the United States. Some who serve at SAFC are former or retired missionaries who know the language of the community and understand the culture. David Echols, a former missionary to Pakistan, has joined with Sam Naaman to create an environment in which visitors feel comfortable. Echols is fluent in Urdu and understands the Asian culture. Naaman commands the respect of his fellow Asians and removes any sense of Western paternalism. But before all else, all attempts to engage our Muslim neighbors must begin with prayer. "With the power of prayer, action should come," Naaman says. "Prayer will take us to the next level."

Small Steps

Americans have their own cultural baggage to overcome. "We are going to have to confront our individualism and space issues," Naaman says. "For people who are going to reach Muslims, those are the things they are going to have to battle." We will also have to battle discouragement. "The only way they're going to find the truth is through individual relationships with Christians who take the time to care—and it's going to take a lot of time," says Kaye, the missionary. "I have heard it said that Muslims have to hear the gospel over one hundred times before the truth of it sinks in. And they have to hear it from different angles, in bits and pieces, until all of a sudden the pieces start falling together. You have to wait for the chances to give them the gospel." Another temptation is to defend the gospel through discussion or argument alone. This frequently does not work with Muslims and often backfires. "They have to defend the honor of Islam," Naaman says.

Kaye adds: "When you get into a conversation with a Muslim, you're better off not getting into an argument. They will win every time because Islam 'has all the answers.' It brags that it does. There's an answer for what to do in any situation."

Effective evangelism among Muslims means incarnating the love of Jesus through friendship, patience, humility, and tenacity. "It comes down to our relationship with Jesus Christ," Kaye says. "That's the only thing they *don't have.*"

Where Do We Begin?

"It is very easy for you to bake a tray of cookies," Naaman says. "Or take her to Wal-Mart. You will spend maybe a dollar on gas. Americans are very gracious. Once they know that this is the way, they will do it."

"Muslim women don't want to sit in their homes and watch TV all day," Kaye says. "Many are lonely and homesick. The women are probably at home and might have trouble with English. They would probably be grateful for a Christian friendship.

"I came to realize that if I wanted to establish communication with my neighbor Hafsa, it was going to have to come from me. I would have preferred to stay in my house to pray about it, but the weight of conviction bore down on me. I put a gold ribbon on a coffee cake I had baked, walked up her front steps, and knocked on the door. Her son answered, but she was close behind. I introduced myself and handed her the coffee cake. "It's my grandmother's recipe," I said. She seemed pleased and surprised and apologized for not calling me.

Hafsa told me how glad she was that my son was talking to Mousa about religion—given what teenagers could be talking about. She showed me a 3-D picture of Jesus and Mary she had hanging on her wall. "I believe in all of the Prophets of God. They are all from God," she said.

We chatted about when she came to the United States from India, and how she once took a part-time job without her husband knowing it. "He speaks several languages—Arabic, Swahili, Zulu, Polish, and he's learning Spanish," she said. She gave me a book about Islam to read and I told her I would read it and get it back to her. She said she would like to have my husband and me over sometime for a meal, or for tea. I told her I would like that.

It was a small step. But the small steps are going to make the difference.

Wendy Murray Zoba is a senior writer for Christianity Today *and the author of several books, including* On Broken Legs: A Shattered Life, a Search for God, a Miracle That Met Me in a Cave in Assisi.

("Engaging Our Muslim Neighbors" was originally published online at www. christianitytoday.com in March 2000.)

For more insightful articles from *Christianity Today* magazine, visit http://www. ctlibrary.com/ and subscribe now.

■ Open Up

Select one of these activities to launch your discussion time.

Option 1

Discuss one of these icebreaker questions:

- How do you generally feel about evangelism? Does the idea of sharing your faith excite you? Make you nervous? Cause you to feel guilty? Describe your gut-reaction.

- Describe any personal interactions you've had with Muslims. Do you have Muslim friends or acquaintances? If so, what is your relationship with them like?

- Off the top of your head, what stands out to you as the main differences between yourself and Muslims you know or have observed in your community? Consider issues of dress, social codes, political views, and so on.

Option 2

For this activity, you'll need toothpicks, drinking straws, masking tape, scissors, and gumdrops.

Slide two similar chairs together so that there is a space of about six to ten inches between them. Your challenge? Work together as a group to design and build a sturdy bridge across the chasm . . . but do it quickly! Take just three minutes to build it.

When you're done, talk about these questions:

• How did your bridge turn out? How could it be improved?

• Do you feel you had enough time to build it? What would you have done if you had more time?

• In what ways can this experience serve as a metaphor for building relationship bridges with Muslims?

■ The Issue

We are called to build a bridge to Muslims in order to bring them back across to Jesus. But this is often not an easy task.

- Why do you think there is such hostility between Muslims and Christians worldwide? Why aren't more organizations like the South Asian Fellowship Center popping up?

- How do you feel about doing cross-cultural ministry with Muslims who may be immigrants who speak a different language, eat different food, or have unique social customs? What would be difficult for you personally about that type of ministry? What do you think might be rewarding for you?

■ Reflect

Please read Luke 10:25–37. Write down anything that stands out to you or questions you may have regarding the passage. Take notes about how this passage speaks to the issue of sharing one's faith with Muslims.

■ Let's Explore

The similarities between Christianity and Islam can be used as a bridge.

Look over the Appendix: "Islam 101," which highlights the main beliefs of Islam, specifically the "Five Tenets" (p.172).

- What are the similarities between the two faiths? How could these similarities be used as starting points on which to build a bridge between the two faiths?

- Now look under the section of Islamic beliefs about Jesus. How would you respond to a Muslim friend who asserted these beliefs? How might you find common ground in order to begin a meaningful discussion?

The Faith Club is a book written by three women—a Muslim, a Jew, and a Christian—describing their friendship and their inter-religious dialogue. Throughout the course of their friendship, the women learned about each other's faiths; ultimately this experience altered their own beliefs as well. The conversations recorded in the book often follow a universalist strain; in their efforts to find common ground, the lines separating the belief systems of the three women became blurry. Here's an excerpt from one of their conversations:

Priscilla: Isn't that blasphemy, Ranya, to say that Islam is just a different version of Judaism and Christianity?

Ranya: No. Not to me. Muslims are required to believe the Gospels and the Torah. Your God is the Muslim God, too.

- What's your reaction to this conversation? If you were Ranya's friend, what might you say to her in response to her statement?

- Imagine a conversation about faith between yourself and a Muslim friend, or think back to a discussion you've had. Where do you draw the line between finding common ground and stressing the differences between your beliefs? Explain.

Your enduring, hospitable friendship with a Muslim is probably the greatest witness that you can have for Jesus.

- Do you think you could develop a meaningful long-term friendship with a Muslim? Or would your fundamental beliefs be so different that you wouldn't be able to truly be close friends? Share your thoughts.

To befriend anyone is to also show them hospitality. Possibly the best example of cross-cultural hospitality in the Bible is the parable of the Good

Samaritan as found in Luke 10:25–37. Revisit this passage, then discuss these questions.

- How does the parable answer the original questions posed to Jesus by the Pharisees in verses 26 and 27?

- What are some of the cultural barriers that often exist between yourself and Muslims? In what ways was this parable cross-cultural? What were the barriers that separated the traveler and the Samaritan?

- What are some ways you could reach out to Muslims to show the same kind of love the Samaritan had for his neighbor? Brainstorm specific ideas together.

Sharing about your relationship with Jesus is a fine balance between being bold and humble.

- One of the principles used by the South Asian Friendship Center is to be bold, strong, and somewhat confrontational in sharing your faith by asserting that Jesus is the only way (John 14:6), as explained by Sam

Naaman. How can this be balanced with the "friendship, patience, humility, and tenacity" that Kaye, the missionary, advises?

- Which evangelism principle is often more challenging to you: being bold or being humble? Why?

- Have you ever tried to share your faith and felt like you were walking the tightrope between being bold and humble at the same time? What was that like for you? For the other person?

- Telling someone that "Jesus is the only way" as the article espouses is, frankly, not "politically correct." How can we push beyond that sense of political incorrectness about Jesus while still being respectful of others?

- Imagine a conversation with a Muslim friend in which you've asserted that salvation through faith in Jesus is the only way to eternal life; you're friend has just contradicted that belief and reasserted his view that Jesus was a prophet. What do you think would be the best way to respond? Why?

■ Going Forward

Take a minute to read and reflect on the following quote from Zoba's article:

Americans have their own cultural baggage to overcome. "We are going to have to confront our individualism and space issues," Naaman says. "For people who are going to reach Muslims, those are the things they are going to have to battle." We will also have to battle discouragement. "The only way they're going to find the truth is through individual relationships with Christians who take the time to care—and it's going to take a lot of time," says Kaye, the missionary. "I have heard it said that Muslims have to hear the gospel over one hundred times before the truth of it sinks in. And they have to hear it from different angles, in bits and pieces, until all of a sudden the pieces start falling together. You have to wait for the chances to give them the gospel."

- From this study and article, do you feel that we need to rethink how we evangelize Muslims? What thoughts or ideas about witnessing to Muslims stand out to you most? Why?

- Building from this study, what are the next few steps you can take to engage your Muslim neighbors? If there are no Muslims in your life right now, how could you use this time to prepare for future friendships?

Spend the last minutes of this study by praying for the Muslims that God has placed in your life or pray that God would bring those of the Islamic faith in your path.

■ Want to Explore More?

Recommended Resources

Answering Islam: The Crescent in the Light of the Cross, Norman L. Geisler and Abdul Saleeb (Baker Books, 2nd Edition, 2002; ISBN 0801064309)

Lifting the Veil: The World of Muslim Women, Phil and Julie Parshall (Authentic, 2002; ISBN 9781884543678)

The Cross and the Crescent: Understanding the Muslim Heart and Mind, Phil Parshall (Stl Distribution, 2002; ISBN 1884543685)

The Koran (Penguin Classics, 2004; ISBN 0140449205)

Unveiling Islam: An Insider's Look at Muslim Life and Beliefs, Ergun Mehmet Caner and Emir Fethi Caner (Kregel Publications, 2002; ISBN 0825424003)

Web Resources:

Answering Islam is an evangelical resource that covers a broad range of topics regarding Islam in great detail (www.answering-islam.org/).

South Asian Friendship Center (www.safc.citymax.com/home.html)

Visit Allied Media Corp. demographic information on American Muslims. (http://www.allied-media.com/AM/index.html).

To see what Muslims in the United States say about themselves, visit: www.theamericanmuslim.org and www.masnet.org.

What do Muslims sacrifice

to follow Christ, and what

can we learn from their

examples?

SCRIPTURE FOCUS

Luke 14:25–33

2 Timothy 3:14–17

THE COST
OF CONVERSION

■

Conversion is a costly decision for Muslims. Choosing
to follow Christ means leaving behind a familiar way
of life, severing relationships with friends and family,
and unlearning everything they once knew about Jesus.
What's worse, Christians are not always eager to welcome
former Muslims into their fellowship. But regardless of the
challenges, former Muslims find true joy and meaning in
their new relationship with Christ.

In this study we will explore how the stories of Ruqaya
in "I Was a Daughter of Islam" and Lamin Sanneh in
"The Defender of the Good News" open our eyes to the
challenges and joys of conversion from Islam to faith
in Christ. Moreover, we'll consider the ways in which
Ruqaya and Lamin challenge *us* to a more faithful
walk with Jesus.

■ Before You Meet

Read "I Was a Daughter of Islam" by Rockie and "The Defender of the Good News: Questioning Lamin Sanneh," an interview by Jonathan Bonk from *Christianity Today* magazine. You may also want to review the appendix, "Islam 101," on p.172.

I WAS A DAUGHTER OF ISLAM

What I discovered when I lifted the veil on my world

By "Rockie"

I was born in Jordan to a Muslim family, and was named Ruqaya after one of the prophet Muhammad's daughters. My uncle, who'd moved to Chicago, told my dad about the wonderful opportunities in the United States, so my dad moved our family here when I was eight years old. While he was excited about providing for his family, my father worried that we'd grow up "Christian." So while my siblings and I went to a public school during the week, we attended Islamic studies on the weekends. The only friends I had were the Muslim kids who attended Islamic studies with me.

As I grew older, my dad became more concerned about the possibility I'd become "Americanized." So when I turned fourteen, my father decided I should return to Jordan to live with my grandmother. I wasn't thrilled about living so far from my family, but when I arrived in Jordan, I loved the people, the culture, and Islam, so I was happy to stay.

More than 90 percent of Muslims are of the Sunni sect—those who strictly follow the Qur'an and the Hadith (the sayings of Muhammad). Since my family was Sunni, I prayed five times a day, fasted during the month of Ramadan, read the Qur'an daily, wore the veil (covering my entire body, and showing only my hands, face, and feet), and tried to imitate the prophet Muhammad in every way. But no matter what I did for Allah, I felt I needed to do more to avoid his wrath. I tried to earn his favor so I could go to heaven.

I spent three years in Jordan, but missed my family so much, I asked my dad if I could return to live with them in the United States. Once I returned, I stopped wearing my head covering because I didn't want to look like an "oddball," but I still kept strong in my prayers and my faith. And I was content—until my father decided it was time for me to get married.

Arab culture dictates men and women are not allowed to date. When a man finds a "suitable" woman, it's usually through family connections. The man and his family visit the young girl's home to meet her family. The "couple" are allowed to speak to each other, but only in the presence of both families. After several similar visits, the couple decide if they want to get married. In Islam, a woman has the right to say no, but in the culture, the family usually pressures the girl to say yes. In both the culture and religion, a woman can marry her first cousin. So when I turned twenty-three, my dad pressured me to marry my first cousin who lives in Jordan. While I was against the marriage and certainly didn't want to spend the rest of my life married to someone I didn't love, I didn't feel I had the choice to go against my father's wishes. My father flew there ahead of me to prepare for the wedding. The rest of my family couldn't afford to fly to Jordan, so my father would be the only immediate family member at the ceremony.

A week later, my elder brother took me to the airport to ensure I got on the plane. Because of tight security on international flights, my brother was unable to take me directly to my gate, so he dropped me off at the main terminal and went home.

As I waited for my flight, I thought about my future. I didn't want to marry my first cousin! But if I didn't, I'd disgrace my family.

In Arab culture, when a woman disgraces her family—or is even rumored to have done so—she deserves to die. I knew if I left the airport and ran away, my family would come after me to kill me for disgracing them. But the longer I thought about how miserable I'd be married to a man I didn't love or respect, the more angry I became. *I've fasted for you; I've prayed five times a day to you; I've even studied the Qur'an for you,* I inwardly screamed at Allah. *And this is what you allow to happen?!* Right then, on February 10, 1990, I stopped praying and worshiping Allah.

I grabbed my luggage and escaped to the nearest hotel to hide. I didn't have much money and desperately tried to think of what to do next. I didn't have many American friends because my father wouldn't allow me to be influenced by their "Satanic ways." But I did know one American woman whom I called from the hotel. I told her briefly what happened and asked if I could stay with her for a while. She came immediately and picked me up.

When the plane landed in Jordan sixteen hours later without me on it, my father became furious. He called my brother and told him to find me.

I stayed with my friend for a few weeks, until one day my brother showed up at her office with a gun. He told her, "I know you have my sister. Give her back before anybody gets hurt!" A coworker called the police, but my brother left before they arrived. My friend got home that night and told me it was too dangerous for me to stay with her any longer, but recommended I stay at a shelter for women suffering from domestic violence.

When I arrived at the shelter, they told me I couldn't stay there either because they'd seen two men showing my photo at a nearby restaurant. They sent me to another shelter an hour away.

After several weeks at that shelter, and only after I began to feel safe, did I allow myself to feel any emotions. Everything I'd bottled up burst out of me, and I sobbed as I mourned the loss of my family and my way of life.

Because I had a naturalized United States citizenship, I joined the National Guard for the government's protection. After my training, I returned and found a job. Miraculously, I hid from my family for four years. But I missed them so much, I finally gathered my courage, contacted my mother, and met with her and my younger sister. We spent most of our time together in tears. The rest of my family had little to say to me. But slowly over time, my family and I began to make peace, and I was amazed at how they finally accepted me back. I thought, *Allah didn't neglect me after all*, and returned to my faith. I didn't pray five times a day or worship him the way I had in the past, but I thanked him daily and did nice things I thought would please him.

In February 1998, I accepted a job for a company based in Texas. Three days after I moved, I met Robyn, who was walking her dog in front of my apartment. We started talking and became fast friends. So when she invited me to go to her church, I agreed. *It's probably okay*, I thought. *My faith believes that Jesus was a messenger of Allah, too. I'm sure Allah won't be upset if I go to church.* I enjoyed the pastor's sermon—except when he talked about Jesus. Sometimes he'd say Jesus is God, and sometimes he'd say Jesus is the Son of God. How could Jesus be both God and God's Son? But I continued to go to church with Robyn until one day the pastor said the church was supporting missionaries in Muslim countries where they don't know Jesus. I thought, *Of course Muslims know Jesus. I need to set the record straight.* After the service, I introduced myself to the pastor, Pete, and said, "I'm a Muslim, and I *do* know Jesus."

I was thoroughly convinced the prophet Muhammad was the last messenger and the Qur'an was the last book sent by Allah. The Qur'an clearly states Jesus was a messenger born of a virgin mother, Mary. He performed many miracles such as bringing the dead to life, healing the sick, speaking when he was a baby, and creating a bird out of clay. Allah loved him so much that when his enemies were preparing to crucify him, he sent someone who looked like Jesus to be crucified instead. Muslims believe Jesus never died, but was raised to heaven to be protected from his enemies. Jesus, in the Qur'an, claims he never told anyone to worship him but to worship the one true God, Allah. According to Muslims, the Bible has been changed—and Christians and Jews don't really have the true books. When Allah gave Muhammad the message, Allah preserved the Qur'an and made sure no one changed it.

The more I attended church, the more I wondered why Christians had different beliefs than Muslims; both the Bible and the Qur'an couldn't be right. As I wrestled with Christianity, I asked Robyn and Pete: Was Jesus crucified? Did Jesus die on the cross for our sins? Is Jesus God, or the Son of God? What is meant by the Trinity? Is the Bible really accurate?

I read different books on Christianity and Islam and discovered the Bible hadn't changed; its books were accurate. Then Pete introduced me to a Bible professor, Dan, who took me through the messianic prophesies of the Old Testament and showed me how they were fulfilled in the New Testament. At that point I was able to believe Jesus was crucified for our sins. But I still wrestled with whether or not Jesus was God. In Islam, to believe in any god other than Allah is blasphemous and unforgivable.

On Sunday, August 2, 1998, several months after I started to investigate Christianity, an Iranian Christian pastor named Iraj, whom I met through Pete, called and said he'd like to meet to discuss our beliefs. That evening, I visited with him and told him I believed in Jesus's crucifixion, but not in his deity. I also told him I'd studied the life of Jesus and no one in history compares to him. Iraj said, "Well, if you think Jesus is that wonderful and that he died on the cross for your sins, will you confess that before God?" I agreed, and we prayed together. That was the day I received Jesus as my Savior. After that, God's Spirit began to open my eyes to the truth of Jesus' deity.

It's been almost four years since that day. My dad and elder sister refuse to speak to me. I maintain a relationship with my mom, who doesn't mention my conversion. My brother rejected me. The rest of my family tolerates my new religion.

One of my deepest longings is to see my family and all Muslims accept Jesus as their Savior and to see Christians burdened for the Muslim people, especially the ones living in the United States.

I'm so grateful Jesus led me to himself. He's been there for me when I needed him—and even when I thought I didn't need him. In Islam, I had to work to earn God's approval. Now I'm free to bask in God's unconditional love! Above all, I'm amazed he loves me so much he died on the cross for me—so that now I'm a daughter of God.

At the time this article was written, "Rockie" was a student majoring in biblical studies.

("I Was a Daughter of Islam" was first published in *Today's Christian Woman*, May/June 2002, Vol. 24, No. 3, Page 29.)

THE DEFENDER OF THE GOOD NEWS: QUESTIONING LAMIN SANNEH

Interview by Jonathan J. Bonk

Lamin Sanneh is the D. Willis James Professor of Missions and World Christianity and professor of history at Yale Divinity School. Gambian born, Sanneh is descended from the nyanchos, an ancient African royal line. As such, his earliest education, in the Gambia, was with fellow chiefs' sons. In this interview with Jonathan J. Bonk, he shares the circumstances of his conversion to Christianity.

What were the circumstances of your early childhood?
I was raised in an orthodox Muslim family and, with the sons of chiefs, went to school in West Africa.

How would your early childhood and adolescence have differed from that of the "typical" North American?
It's like living on another planet. I was raised in a culture where the stress is not on the individual but on the community, on tradition, on fidelity to past models, on respect for parents and elders, on rote memorization of knowledge, on scarce material resources offset by a wealth of social capital. We had limited access to the modern world, but lavish access to family and clan achievement and honor. We had close proximity to the natural world without the demand to subdue and exploit it. One could go on.

What made you interested in Christianity?
Reading about Jesus in the Qur'an piqued my curiosity. I had no access to the Bible or to a church at the time, and so the Qur'an remained the authoritative and only source of Jesus, son of Mary (the respectful form the Qur'an uses).

Did you express this curiosity openly?
By force of circumstance, I kept counsel with myself. My teachers would react unpredictably, and my Muslim friends would be scandalized.

Were any of your teachers or fellow classmates similarly curious?
Yes, but they lacked my effrontery, perhaps.

How difficult was it to convert from Islam to Christianity?

Once the choice was made about the significance of Jesus in God's work of salvation, it was not difficult to make the decision to join the church. Getting accepted in the Protestant church, however, was a different matter altogether, thanks to the church's suspicion and skepticism. It is only now, at long last, in the Catholic Church that I feel accepted unconditionally and unreservedly. It vindicates my view that faith counts for something, though it was a long time coming.

Did you find that Christians welcomed you with open arms once you had declared your desire to convert?

On the contrary. The church was suspicious and distrustful.

Could you elaborate just a little more on that point?

Unofficially, the Methodist church in question welcomed my decision to seek baptism, but officially they put off the decision to baptize me.

They asked instead that I to go to the Catholic Church, which I did for a year, but with the same result, I found.

The Catholics also appeared reluctant, and suspicious, too, it seemed. I had hit an ecumenical obstacle. In mitigation, the Methodist church assured me that their baptism, when they did it, would be recognized by the Catholic Church. I expressed relief at what seemed like hedging your bets and doubling the favorable odds at the same time. It still took two years to accomplish the object in view, and only because I gave an ultimatum, though the Methodist church added the precaution of readings on New Testament form criticism for my catechism. Away with any risk of the Bible being taken, like the Qur'an, as the impeccable word of God!

That precaution of a rational, progressive understanding of Christianity appeared to have failed when, with my interest still obviously undiminished, I requested to be allowed to study theology. I received a swift negative response, with the indication that their decision was backed by the mission headquarters in London (in case I harbored a stubborn thought I had any remaining support there).

Those were the ungarnished facts that I as a very young convert had to deal with (or not deal with, if I chose). It happened that I was so profoundly affected by the message of Jesus, so inexplicably transformed at the roots of faith and trust, that I felt myself in the grips of an undeniable impetus to give myself to God, whatever my ultimate career path. I never had cause to fret about the work to which God might call me; so steadfast are God's promises.

Following your conversion, what did you most miss about Islam?

I am not sure "miss" is the right word, but I acquired a deep appreciation for Islam, for its sense of divine transcendence, for my own formation in its moral milieu, for the habits of obedience and faithfulness it transcribed in me, and for the idea it inculcated of the truth and reality of God in human affairs. We should remember that while God and Jesus are swear words in the West, that is not so in the Muslim world. People would never take the name of God and God's prophets in vain. We need a dose of Islam's reverence to keep us honest about our own faith. We need each other if for no other reason.

What role, if any, did Western missionaries play in your conversion, either directly or indirectly?

I never went to a mission school and knew no missionaries at all when I embarked on my inquiry. It was only later, after I moved to the capital city, that I met English teachers at a government school. So missionaries played little role in my conversion experience.

Why did you finally move into communion with the Roman Catholic Church, after your long sojourn as a Protestant?

The Catholic Church eventually relented after years of ignoring and wishing me away! In that time the Protestant church had remained for the most part incredulous of me.

I do not know the reason for that. It could be cultural, it could be liberal distrust of religion, it could be residual hostility toward converts as illegitimate fruits of mission, it could be unfamiliarity with non-white people, it could be presumptions about my political motives and leanings, it could be any or all of the above, how do I know. But, whatever it was, it wore me down eventually.

I felt my reasons for being a Christian had little resonance with the reasons a liberal West gives for the Christian name. I remember on a visit to Germany from Africa when I was on school vacation seeing the sign, "The Episcopal Church Welcomes You," and duly betaking myself there one Sunday only to discover I was unwelcome! My secular white American friend felt vindicated about why he ceased to be a practicing

Christian. It was all one big cultural pretense, he said. Don't get literal with Christian slogans. There would be no questions asked if I was white, he observed caustically.

I realized that a cultural paradigm had usurped the place of God in our enlightened scheme of things, and that was one reason why for so long the church tried to make me feel guilty and untrustworthy for claiming the Christian name. With my religious orientation, however, I was unable to reconcile myself to that fundamental compromise with the world. I thought Jesus was for real in spite of the prevarications of the church.

How would you describe the present state of your relationships with your immediate and extended Muslim families?

It is a complicated one. The African members of my extended family have little conception of my world, little idea of the milieu of my life and work and the expanding network of friends and colleagues spread across the world. For many of them, the West is the land of riches, and so it appears implausible to them that anyone could be said to be successful who was not successful in the financial sense. I am often tempted to lecture them about mortgages, college tuition, about the insurance Leviathan that engulfs home, car, body, limb and teeth, about fuel and utility bills, or about Uncle Sam's long and heavy hands on our wages and our spending. An occasionally sympathetic listener might say perceptively, 'but you don't own yourself anymore,' but otherwise it is a futile exercise. The love of money is a universal desire, admittedly, but being in America turns it into a prerequisite. It trumps everything else.

It is impossible to overcome such expectations about being successful in America, but continuing family demands require an ongoing relationship unconstrained by that. So I have maintained contact, with the occasional visit and exchange of news.

How does your experience play into your understanding of Muslim-Christian dialogue?

The responsibility of the church to respond positively to the Muslim challenge I see as constitutive of the Christian response to God. I remain convinced that the church will emerge renewed and revitalized from that challenge.

What do you think about current missionary efforts to evangelize Muslims?

I am sure evangelizing Muslims will make more of an impression on the Christian evangelizers themselves than on the Muslim world. Given the extent of indifference and complacency about the religious life among Christians, it is perhaps a good thing if they are shaken out of that torpor, however circuitous the path by which they arrive at that awakening. Muslims will continue to pay them scant attention.

What are among the most serious misunderstandings that Muslims typically hold regarding Christians?

Several misunderstandings leap to mind at random. Muslims believe that Christians:

have no revealed language for revelation and so are divided by the languages of the world;

deny the oneness of God by their trinity;

labor under the misapprehension that Jesus was crucified when, according to the Qur'an, he was not;

without a mandate like the *salât* of Islam, follow their own whim in the worship of God;

have no revealed law and so cannot know or follow the truth;

blaspheme when they call Jesus the Son of God instead of the son of Mary, as Muslims say;

have abandoned the Mosaic code on dietary practice and the Sabbath;

are unfaithful to the teachings of God's prophets, including those of Jesus, concerning obedience and unity of faith and practice;

are in error when they separate church and state with the goal of reducing religion to the private and subjective level;

have turned to the nation state as an object of worship and for which they give their lives;

give citizenship and patriotism primacy over allegiance to God;

promote religion as personal, emotional assurance without reference to society and the world, as if it is enough to say religion is grace, which is nothing other than religion as a vague, general aspiration without the means or method to implement it, or the space to practice it;

practice a religion that is without a home or a promise land, and so have little respect for Islam as a religion at home still in its birth-place while prevailing in many other places besides.

How is the Muslim faith most frequently misunderstood in the West?

Comparable misunderstandings of Islam in the West include the beliefs that Islam:

is a violent religion that breeds terror;

is intolerant of other religions;

oppresses women;

is a religion of laws and rules rather than of grace;

uses jihad to spread itself;

unites church and state to breed intolerance, fanaticism, and conflict;

restricts revelation to a book instead of to a person;

was founded by a man who used violence as a weapon;

encourages polygamy.

Lamin Sanneh is the D. Willis James Professor of Missions and World Christianity and professor of history at Yale Divinity School. Following graduation from the University of London with a Ph.D. in Islamic History, he taught at the University of Ghana and at the University of Aberdeen, in Scotland. He served for eight years as assistant and associate professor of the History of Religion at Harvard University, before moving to Yale University in 1989. The author of a dozen books and scores of articles, he is an editor-at-large for The Christian Century *and a contributing editor for the* International Bulletin of Missionary Research.

Jonathan Bonk is the executive director of the Overseas Ministries Study Center, editor of the International Bulletin of Mission Research, *and project director for the* Dictionary of African Christian Biography.

("The Defender of the Good News" was originally published in full in *Christianity Today*, October 2003.)

For more insightful articles from *Christianity Today* magazine, visit http://www.ctlibrary.com/ and subscribe now.

■ Open Up

Choose one of the following activities to launch your discussion time.

Option 1

Discuss one of these icebreaker questions:

- Reflect on a time that a new relationship with a roommate, spouse, or friend required you to give up something you loved—whether a pet, a hobby, a habit, or a favorite recliner. How did you feel about that sacrifice? Why did you make it?

- Now imagine you've moved to a different country with a completely different culture. What are some "comforts of home" you'd have a very hard time giving up? Brainstorm several together, such as foods, favorite items, special places, or other comforts.

- Of all the comforts of home you discussed, which one comfort would be most difficult for you to give up? Why?

Option 2

For this activity, every group member should make a list of the most valuable things in their lives—the things that are worth the most. Their lists should include material things, but also relationships, hobbies, interests . . . whatever they value most. Take a few minutes to finish the lists, then come back together as a group.

Jim Elliot, a 19th Century Christian and martyr said, "He is no fool who gives up what he cannot keep to gain what he cannot lose."

- Take a look at your list again, what are the things on this list that you cannot keep? How hard would it be for you to give up those things for your faith?

- What about the people and relationships on the list—would you be willing to give those up to follow Jesus? How does that make you feel?

- When it comes to faith in Jesus, there is a cost. Most of us haven't had to give up relationships or even material things to follow Jesus, but there are those who have. Describe a situation you've heard of in which the cost of following Jesus was very high.

■ The Issue

"I Was a Daughter of Islam" and "The Defender of the Good News" both recount an experience of conversion from Islam to Christianity. Both Ruqaya and Lamin found ultimate fulfillment in their new relationships with Christ, but they also faced extraordinary challenges when they left Islam to follow Jesus.

- What sacrifices did Ruqaya and Lamin make to become followers of Christ?

- What things did—and do—*you* sacrifice to follow Jesus?

■ Reflect

Take a moment to read Luke 14:25–33 and 2 Timothy 3:14–17 on your own and jot down a few notes and observations about the passages. What do you find surprising or interesting about these passages? What questions do these passages raise? Note any ways you think these verses relate to the experiences of Ruqaya and Lamin.

■ Let's Explore

Faith for Muslims and Christians alike is profoundly cultural.
In her article, Ruqaya explains that although her father was eager to move his family to the United States, he was also concerned that they might become "Americanized" and "Christian"—as if those terms are interchangeable.

• What about American culture might lead Muslims to believe that to be American is to be Christian?

• Can you recall a time when you realized that you believed or acted a certain way because you were an American rather than because you were a Christian? Share that experience with the group.

In his interview, Lamin argues that American Christians have made a "fundamental compromise with the world" and are, as a result, culturally captive.

• In what ways might Christianity be culturally captive in America? How might the perceived relationship between being American and being Christian be a hindrance to Muslim conversion?

Family relationships are profoundly significant for both Muslims and Christians. Review Luke 14:25–27 together.

- In what ways did Ruqaya and Lamin experience the truth of this passage? Under what circumstances might this passage apply to Christians in America?

Revisit all of Luke 14:25–33. Like a builder assessing the cost of building a tower, each person must honestly consider the stark realities of the costs of following Jesus. This is not a popular evangelism method in our world—but Jesus wanted to make sure people knew that following him would mean giving up a lot.

- What are the costs of conversion to Christianity for a Muslim? Brainstorm as many as you can think of. How are these costs like or unlike the costs of discipleship in your own life?

Muslim converts must learn to understand Jesus in a new way.

Ruqaya and Lamin both encountered Jesus first through the Qur'an. What impressions of Jesus did they develop through Islam? How did these impressions make conversion difficult? How might they have aided their conversion? (Feel free to reference "Islam 101: Basics of a Foreign Faith" in the appendix.)

Ruqaya and Lamin were not the only people with misconceptions about Jesus. Sometimes those who have been Christians the longest have the hardest time seeing Jesus as he really is. Theologian and pastor N. T. Wright has the following to say about Christian discipleship in *The Challenge of Jesus*:

The disciplines of prayer and Bible study need to be rooted again and again in Jesus himself if they are not to become idolatrous or self-serving. We have often muted Jesus's stark challenge, remaking him in our own image and then wondering why our personal spiritualities have become less than exciting and life-changing.

- In what ways do you sometimes remake Jesus in your own image? How does the Bible's portrayal of Jesus challenge you most?

While the Qur'an presents a false view of Jesus, our Old Testament provides a great deal of information about him. Read 2 Timothy 3:14–17 together. Keep in mind that when Paul uses the word *Scripture,* he's referring to the Old Testament.

- Can you think of one Old Testament passage or story that helps you better understand Jesus? Share what it means to you.

■ Going Forward

Take another look in the article at Lamin's list of misunderstandings that Muslims typically hold about Christians.

- Which of these do you find most challenging? Why?

- How do we contribute to these misunderstandings? What steps can we take to correct these misunderstandings?

Break into pairs to discuss this final question:

- Lamin and Ruqaya are both heroes of the faith, for they counted the cost of discipleship and chose to be faithful against incredible odds. How have their stories personally encouraged you to be a more faithful follower of Christ?

Pray for one another in pairs, asking that you may each have the courage to follow Lamin and Ruqaya in radical obedience. Commit to pray for each other every day this week.

■ Want to Explore More?

Recommended Resources

The Challenge of Jesus: Rediscovering Who Jesus Was and Is, N. T. (Tom) Wright (InterVarsity Press, 1999; ISBN-10 0830822003)

The Cost of Discipleship, Dietrich Bonhoeffer (Touchstone; 1st Touchstone Ed, 1995; ISBN-10 0684815001)

How to Read the Bible for All Its Worth, Gordon D. Fee (Zondervan; 3rd Revised Ed, 2003; ISBN-10 0310246040)

"I Believe": Exploring the Apostles' Creed, Alister McGrath (InterVarsity Press, 1998; ISBN-10 0830819460)

Understanding the Koran: A Quick Christian Guide to the Muslim Holy Book, Mateen Elass (Zondervan, 2004; ISBN-10 0310248124)

■ Appendix

Islam 101: Basics of a Foreign Faith
(from *Christian History & Biography* magazine; April 1, 2002)

The Five Pillars of Islam

Shahadah: Confession of faith. "There is no God but Allah, and Muhammad is His messenger."

Salat: Prayer. All Muslims are to pray five times every day, facing Mecca.

Zakat: Tithing. Muslims must give at least 2.5 percent of their total wealth to the poor and needy.

Sawm: Fasting. During the holy month of Ramadan, Muslims are to refrain from food, water, and sex from sunrise to sunset.

Hajj: Pilgrimage. If at all possible, at least once in a lifetime Muslims are to travel to Mecca to engage in rituals of prayer and worship at the central shrine in Islam's holiest city.

The Qur'an

The Qur'an, in Arabic, is the perfect Word of Allah.

The Qur'an contains 114 chapters, or suras.

Muslims believe that the Qur'an was revealed to Muhammad by the archangel Gabriel.

The Qur'anic material was composed from 610 through Muhammad's death in 632.

The final compilation was completed about 650.

The Prophet

Most Muslims believe that Muhammad was sinless, but not divine.

Most Muslims believe that the prophet was illiterate.

The prophetic status of Muhammad is not to be questioned.

Muhammad provides the greatest example for all aspects of life.

The traditions about the prophet are known as *hadith*.

Allah gave the prophet permission to have twelve wives.

Other Major Muslim Beliefs

Islam started with Adam, not with Muhammad.

People are saved by the will of God through obedience to God's law, *Shari'ah*.

Though humans are imperfect, they are not fallen through original sin.

Those chosen by God for salvation will enter Paradise. Only God knows whom he has chosen.

The damned will burn in eternal torment in Hell.

All countries and peoples should follow Islam and Islamic law.

Muslims are to engage in *jihad*, which usually means private spiritual struggle.

Jihad sometimes demands defense of Muslim territory and military aggression.

God will restore the world at the end of time through a coming human leader known as the *Mahdi*.

Muslim males can marry up to four wives.

Muslim Groups

Almost 90 percent of Muslims belong to the *Sunni* tradition.

Shi'ite Islam is popular in Iran, Iraq, Lebanon, Syria, and several Persian Gulf states.

Sufi Islam represents the mystical path.

The Islam practiced in most Muslim countries is heavily influenced by local folk customs.

Muslim Views of Jesus

Jesus was a prophet of God but not the Son of God. He was a lesser prophet than Muhammad.

He was born of the virgin Mary.

He performed many miracles.

He was protected from a death of crucifixion.

He did not rise from the dead.

He ascended to heaven after his death, and he will return to earth.

He was a faithful Muslim, or follower of Allah.

Bonus Small-Group Builder

From SmallGroups.com

You can find more helpful insights for small group health at
www.smallgroups.com.

This study includes discussions and Scripture passages that are sure to challenge assumptions or opinions group members may have about Islam. You may, in fact, discover that by the end of your time exploring this topic, you've changed your mind about how you perceive Islam or how you desire to relate to Muslim friends and neighbors. This insightful article for small groups from Dan Lentz, Director of the Small Group Network, will help you process these challenges together.

CHANGING PEOPLE'S MINDS

By Dan Lentz

Have you ever changed your mind about something? I have changed my mind more about things in the last few years than I would ever have dreamed I would. Here is a very humbling experience of that from my own life. When I started working in industry, I had the idea that a person should not miss work for anything, particularly when you were sick. So for six plus years straight, I never missed a day of work because of illness. Did I get sick during that time? Yes. But I said, "no matter, I'm going to work."

That line of thinking started to spill over into how I viewed other people. I had friends at work at that time who got sick and missed a day of work every month or two. I became convinced they had the wrong values, and that they were either uncommitted, lazy, or just wimpy. I realized that everyone has times when they don't feel good, but I always felt that if a person is committed enough, they can still make it to work. At least, that's what I thought then.

But then, I started to change my mind.

Why? Over time, I got some information from those people who missed work frequently that helped me understand why they struggle to make it to work when certain health conditions were a problem. Still, even though the information helped, down deep, I was still doubtful that they really needed to be off work as much as they were.

But then something really caused me to change my mind. I got a chronic illness. The guy who thought anyone who let illness interrupt everyday life was just a wimp, became chronically sick, and stayed chronically sick. And it did interrupt everyday life. It did make work and normal activity impossible at times. I got it. I changed my mind.

So what does it take to change your mind?

Knowledge about something can change a person's mind, but what really tends to change minds is knowledge coupled with a related experience. We can have a lot of information that would lead us in a direction to change our minds, but knowledge of the truth doesn't always tip us until we have a relevant experience.

True mind change, in a spiritual context, is called transformation (Romans 12:2). When does transformation happen? Does transformation happen when we receive information regarding biblical truth? Sometimes. My experience has been that biblical truth is very important to the transformation process, but even though I said a truth had changed my mind, my actions didn't always flesh that out. When biblical information or knowledge alone does not truly change our mind, does not truly transform us, then what does? Sometimes we need to know the truth and experience the truth as well (James 2:17). Real application of a truth is where life change happens—not just talking about application, but living the application.

Academic or informational Bible studies in small groups can be important, but if you are not living out or experiencing the truths of those studies together in community, your small group members may not be changing their minds as much as you think.

So how can small groups help change people's minds? Here are some suggestions:

- Always allot a significant amount of time to focus on application of any study you are doing. At least half of any "lesson" time should focus specifically on application.

- Don't make application theoretical. In other words, glean as many personal specific examples of application as you can, including past victories and defeats when applying biblical truth. Encourage and spur one another on in these examples.

- Be intentional about planning experiences into group life: service projects, prayer walks, confession exercises, hospital visits, etc.

- Discern specific areas where transformation is slow and plan experiences around those areas. Example: Several small group members are having trouble loving people of a different ethnicity, so plan a time when they can serve those of that different ethnicity.

- Draw the connection or ask questions about how God is using specific circumstances to transform your group members. Example question: How is God using your current suffering to change your mind about things?

- Recognize and celebrate times when people acknowledge that they have changed their mind at deeper levels about deeply held issues.

- Pray the Holy Spirit would be constantly renewing the minds of your small group members.

Remember that changing a mind goes beyond knowledge. It requires knowing the right things and living those things as well. Don't let your small group settle for only knowing the right things.